About the Author

Raised in a working-class family in Southeast London during the 1950s and 1960s, Brian Holloway attended the Roger Manwood Comprehensive School before embarking on a career in the finance and commercial sectors of Industry. He subsequently worked with the Civil Service for forty-one years, mostly in procurement, before retiring due to an increasing hearing loss, a disability he had contended with from an early age.

Reflecting on his childhood, he recalls at the age of nine narrowly escaping a fatal accident when two cars collided at a crossroad junction at the bottom of a steep hill, causing a black Jaguar to somersault several times before coming to rest barely a few yards in front him. Is it possible that the course of his life could have changed on that day through a small intervention by those who are known to accompany him throughout his life?

He is married to Rita, who comes from a family of spiritual mediums, with whom he has worked on *A Collection of Conversations with Spirits*. They have travelled together extensively and share a deep connection through their lives as soul mates, having been together for over fifty years in this existence.

"Qn: You are a new visitor, why are you here?"
"Visitor: I am here to experience the whole physical movement of the drum. I am sure that you will see that I am quite accomplished at this. I am enjoying the ability to communicate so freely and quickly. I feel it is quite freeing and not dependent on someone translating my words and often changing them as they cannot listen to a full conversation like I can have with you now."

"Qn: What is the Light?"
"Chief: The Light is filled with love and is like an experience you will never have quite come across in this physical existence."

"Qn: …. still, it will keep you on your toes. Sorry, I didn't mean to say that as you don't have feet."
"CP: I have spirit toes."

"Qn: But you don't walk, you float, don't you?"
"CP: No, I walk in spirit."

"Qn: How do you walk in the spirit world?"
"CP: It is a solid vibration range we exist in. Like you exist in your vibration range."

"Qn: I had not realised it is the same for you in your existence, as it is in this physical existence."
"CP: We float in your range because we vibrate faster."

A COLLECTION OF

Conversations with Spirits

Intuitive Questions and Answers about Spirit

BRIAN HOLLOWAY

SilverWood

Published in 2025 by SilverWood Books

SilverWood Books Ltd
14 Small Street, Bristol, BS1 1DE, United Kingdom
www.silverwoodbooks.co.uk

Copyright © Brian Holloway 2025

The right of Brian Holloway to be identified as the author of this
work has been asserted in accordance with the Copyright,
Designs and Patents Act 1988 Sections 77 and 78.

All rights reserved. No part of this publication may be reproduced,
stored in a retrieval system, or transmitted in any form or by any means,
electronic, mechanical, photocopying, recording or otherwise,
without prior permission of the copyright holder.

ISBN 978-1-80042-310-7 (paperback)
Also available as an ebook

British Library Cataloguing in Publication Data
A CIP catalogue record for this book is available from the British Library

Page design and typesetting by SilverWood Books

NO AI TRAINING
Without in any way limiting the author's exclusive rights under copyright, any use of this publication to train generative artificial intelligence (AI) technologies to generate text is expressly prohibited. The author reserves all rights to license uses of this work for generative AI training and development of machine learning language models.

*I dedicate this book to my loving partner Rita
and our spirit Guides
Thank you for working together and giving your time to
provide so much knowledge and insight into the spirit world.*

*The publication of the many transcripts of conversations has
only been made possible by the willingness of
our spirit Guides to share these treasured insights into
where we come from, what we are, and where we will
eventually return home to.*

*To my Children
Dejihnita:e'*

*For my Children and Grandchildren:
Quelli che ti hanno amato nella vita, ti amano di piu dal
mondo degli spiriti
(those who have loved you in life, love you more from
the spirit world)*

*To Family, Friends and Visitors (and not forgetting
those who have already returned home)
I extend heartfelt gratitude for your support to
the Library Circle over many years
You know who you are –
Thank you for helping to share in the many experiences
with our spirit friends*

Contents

Preface	9
A Journey in Life	12
Section 1	
Communication	15
Guides, Spirits (and IDs)	34
Section 2	
The Source and Spirit World	53
The Realms	83
The Light	88
Transitioning between Worlds	111
Earthbound Spirits	134
Higher Conscious	150
Visitors from the Past	167
Karma	180
A *Physical* Life Path	183
Energy and Bumps and Bangs	188
General Questions	194
Conundrum	200
Other Life in the Universe	204

Preface

The conversations documented in this publication took place in a room that had been adapted into a modest library within a typical suburban home. The group who met to experience the channelling of these conversations became known as the Library Circle and the first sitting occurred in 2013. Over the years, the Library Circle has been visited by various individual spirits and entities from the spirit world seeking to make their presence known, as well as by those 'physical' visitors who shared an interest in communicating with the spirit world or wanted to satisfy their curiosity on the existence of an afterlife. The main objective of the Library Circle was to collect evidence and obtain information regarding the afterlife by engaging in regular communication with spirits. Although there are extensive writings on personal spiritual experiences by various authors, at the outset of this journey, I was unsure where this path would lead or whether there would be any success in fulfilling this endeavour. I most certainly had not anticipated that this journey would result in me maintaining recordings of the Circle sittings and transcribing the many informative and insightful conversations for inclusion in this publication. People have described me as having an inquisitive nature, regularly questioning, reasoning, challenging, and searching for truth. After many years, I discovered it.

I started out with very little knowledge about the spirit world or where it was and even questioned whether there is an afterlife. However, I had been privileged to have married into a family that, over several generations, exhibited strong spiritual and mediumship skills. It was after nearly 40 years of marriage, that I finally agreed to assist my lifelong partner Rita to rekindle the spiritual mediumship skills that she possessed and had always been encouraged by her parents from a very early age never to ignore. Of course, I quickly realised that I would have to earn the trust of those in spirit before they would be willing to share with us so much knowledge about their own lives in spirit. And more recently, would I be able to do them justice by publishing their responses to the many inquisitive questions posed by the Circle. After many years, I think I have been able to.

Many books have been written that offer readers spiritual knowledge, messages and experiences, all with the good intention of sharing evidence and teachings about the afterlife. So, why should the conversations published in this book be any different? This book aims to present what I believe to be a unique perspective for readers to share in information that has been transcribed from many recordings and avoids any direct religious or cultural influence – although I did learn that faith does still occur in spirit.

As I have said, when I started gathering this information, I did not possess any credible spiritual knowledge until I had commenced recording these conversations that the Circle was having with many spirit visitors. I have tried hard not to offend or question other cultures or faiths, my sole objective being to explore with spirits a range of practical questions that only they are able to answer, including some questions about their lives and what can be expected when it is eventually our turn to return home to spirit. I have not included any questions and answers that might pertain to faith or cultural beliefs unless such a response was integral to the spirit's answer.

Over the years, the Library Circle, fostered and supported the development of several Mediums and Healers and provided those 'physical' visitors attending the various demonstrations with their own opportunity to decide for themselves whether an afterlife exists. We never presented fake sessions, and on the rare occasion of inactivity, then this would be acknowledged without issue, and we would move on to the next sitting a few days later. Neither did we seek at any time to charge fees or receive financial contribution from any 'physical' visitors when attending any of the sittings held.

Your journey in a physical life is unique and frequently involves learning from mistakes and achievements; I have experienced many of both. It is not my intent for the contents of this book to persuade you to change your life, you are free to make your own choices and decisions based upon your own beliefs. But I do ask you to keep an open mind when reading these transcripts as these insights will enhance your own awareness and understanding of the afterlife and provide a deeper understanding of our origins and place in the Universe.

This book is a compilation of information attained from transcripts of the Library Circle's conversations with visitors from the spirit world gathered over many years. To the best of my knowledge, these conversations provide a narrative of genuine and insightful knowledge concerning the afterlife and some of the potential experiences that an individual might encounter when returning home to the spirit world.

The conversations transcribed in this book are questions about life in the spirit world with answers narrated by many spirit visitors. <u>These answers have either been channelled through deep trance mediumship or by spirits using physical energy to write their answers by movement of a physical object. Who would be more knowledgeable about the afterlife in the spirit world than the spirits themselves?</u>

A Journey in Life

As you read through *A Collection of Conversations with Spirits* you may come to understand, as I have, that life is a journey we undertake each time we come down to the physical realm. Each new journey that is undertaken may occur by personal choice or invitation, however throughout this journey many lessons will be learned and mistakes made, new individuals will be encountered, and valuable familial relationships as well as new friendships will be established or renewed. For each new journey that is navigated, everyone will encounter various phases of life that will shape or re-shape their personality. Childhood innocence will gradually give way to adolescent curiosity, and the excitement of youth will blossom into the responsibilities of adulthood. Each journey will be marked by personal growth, self-discovery, learning, and eventually the evolution of an individual's beliefs and perspectives. And all these things will accompany you into your eternal spiritual existence in spirit, allowing you to determine how you decide how you may wish to continue living your eternal existence in spirit.

Throughout my journey in this life, I had found myself questioning the nature of reality and the possible existence of realms beyond the physical world and this intensified as my relationship with Rita progressed beyond courtship to marriage. Especially as Rita comes from a family deeply rooted in spiritual mediumship that includes grandmother, mother, father, sister, uncles, aunts, cousins, and this familial tradition has also extended to our children and there are early signs of this continuing.

Life took a significant turn in 2012 after I had retired, when Rita told me she felt she was being called upon to re-awaken her spiritual mediumship skills to reconnect with her true calling and life journey. I agreed to help despite having little knowledge of the subject. Despite the significant family involvement with spirit, for many years I had chosen not to become involved with this family tradition, as I did not understand how science and spirit were able to co-exist together in the 21st century. Nevertheless, our children had left home, and we had a lot of spare time to explore something completely new together, so why not try something outside the norm. A spare room was prepared where Rita could meditate quietly, and it was not too long before she began entering deeper trance states while I observed and ensured all was well.

Eventually, spirits started to surprise me as they utilised the deep trance states they could achieve with Rita and began communicating through her, and it was not long after that several spirit Guides introduced themselves and identified others who would be collaborating with us as we got to know each other better. A few months later, the Library Circle was established.

It was several years into this journey that a spirit you will come to know as the Chief introduced himself and brought into play the use of physical energy as an alternative means for spirit communication. This grew to have more appeal to me, as it also enabled spirits to communicate visually with their audience by movement of objects and this became the point where I started to understand how science and spirit do co-exist together and enabled the unwavering belief that I now have.

In 2018, my spirit Guides suggested that I might want to try publishing some of the regular conversations we were having.

Although I had kept recordings of these compelling discussions, I had not considered writing a book. Becoming an author posed a challenge for me as I did not believe I possessed the literary skills necessary to undertake such a project. However, upon further reflection, I decided to attempt creating something for publication that might interest readers who are curious and want to understand more about the spirit world, the afterlife, and events that follow death.

Thanks to the on-going help from spirit Guides and those new spirit friendships that have been made, I am able to present the afterlife **as it truly is**.

Section 1

Communication

Communication is an integral aspect of our daily lives. If I wanted to learn more about the existence of an afterlife in the spirit world then establishing a genuine communication channel with spirits was the first challenge that needed to be overcome.

Human speech is generated by air passing from the lungs through vocal chords which vibrate to create the sound of the human voice. However, how can we effectively communicate with an unseen presence that we can only believe is there listening to us, and how might that unseen presence be able to communicate with us? In the physical world, technology uses radio waves to facilitate long-distance communication with a person we cannot see. These radio waves are converted into mechanical vibrations, which generate sound waves that can be detected by human ears. Furthermore, individuals with speech or hearing impairments have overcome their physical disabilities by utilising sign language, lip reading or use various other forms of advanced technological aids designed for hearing or speech that will meet the specific needs of an individual.

When a spirit attempts to communicate a message to a person in the physical realm, what methods do they use? Additionally, how do spirits interact and communicate amongst themselves within the spirit realm?

Inevitably, communicating with an unseen or unknown party inherently presents challenges, as it introduces uncertainty about whether the intended audience will be engaged. Some Mediums claim to have the ability to be able to see or communicate with spirits and offer their services as intermediaries to relay messages from spirits to those in the physical world who are willing to listen.

I do not lay any claim to be a Medium because, despite many attempts with personal meditation, I have not been able to initiate mental communication directly with spirit. Unfortunately, I just do not seem to possess what it takes to channel in such a way as a spiritual Medium is able to. Nevertheless, having a partner who is a highly skilled spiritual Medium has been extremely beneficial, particularly as she is someone who spirits seem able to communicate with or channel through at their ease. Although I may not possess this ability myself, communication with spirits appears to be a distinguishing characteristic that has persisted through Rita's family and has continued to flow down through our family.

So, how did we go about opening a communication channel with spirits? Well, I can say that the process required considerable time, effort and patience on our part, because it was some time before spirits could converse as freely with the Circle sittings as they do today. These Circle sittings are generally held in a dimly lit room, with calming and soothing music played for around thirty minutes prior to the commencement of each session as part of the preparation. The duration of a sitting is governed by a pre-defined time limit[1], established at the outset by using a pre-prepared playlist of music that is played for the duration of each sitting and the closing track signals the end of the session. Each sitting began with an opening request

---

1   Setting a time limit for Circle sittings will ensure that they do not last longer than you might want it to. In later Sections, you will learn that the spirit world has no concept of time. In the physical world, time is governed by the passing of 24-hour days and Earth cycles around the Sun which are used to organise and measure our lives.

or behest setting out the intent of the session and specifying the purpose or objective that we hoped to accomplish, albeit what happened was usually at the behest of the visiting spirits. Each sitting concluded with a closing request to facilitate the 'physical' participants returning to their normal physical state.

In the early stages of the Circle sittings, visiting spirits would often utilise transfigurations to demonstrate their presence or manipulated the energy they had created in various ways to interact with Circle members whilst developing trance mediumship with the sitting Medium. These were always entertaining to watch as various spirits transfigured the Medium by presenting a continuous stream of individual spirit faces within the grey energy that was superimposed over of the sitting Medium's face. At other times, spirits would occasionally display hazy objects or shapes of animals within these clouds or generated small sparks of energy that seemed to emanate from between the Medium's hands. This practice continued for several years, enabling physical participants and spirits to build mutual confidence.

The communication methods used by the Circle are similar to those used by other Mediums who are able to interact with spirits. Most Mediums describe the messages they receive from spirits as being akin to a telepathic implant in their minds and, unless the message is intended for the Medium, it is conveyed to the intended recipient. Additionally, a spirit may implant visual images into the mind of a Medium who will then describe these visuals to the audience or recipient. These two methods appear to be the most frequently used methods of communication employed by spirits when communicating with the physical world.

An alternative and more complex method of communication used by spirits involves the spiritual Medium entering into a deep trance state, thereby allowing a spirit to use the Medium's vocal chords to deliver messages directly to the intended audience. However, the reasons for spirits being able to carry out this form of communication through certain Mediums while not others remain unclear, but I hoped that spirits will solve that question for me.

These traditional methods of communication have probably been practiced by spirits and spiritual Mediums for generations and can be considered a significant aspect of how spirits convey the existence of an afterlife. The Library Circle has utilised all the aforementioned methods of communication when interacting with spirits. Just as development happens in the physical world, so it must also be a possibility that spirits will also progress with their own development and find more effective ways to communicate with the physical world in the future, although the methods of communication mentioned in this Section are working effectively for this Circle. As spirits are more knowledgeable about the processes involved in each of the communication methods being used, they will be best able to further describe them.

This Section contains information about the conversations the Circle had with a number of spirits, including the Chief and an entity referred to as the Conglomerate. Further details about these spirits, and other spirits and Guides can be found in the next Section.

Communication – Use of Transfigurations

Qn: In the very early days of the Circle, spirits demonstrated their existence using transfigurations. We continue to view transfigurations in red light, but how do you do it? How do you prepare the Medium to show the transfigurations?

Chief: There are the steps to be followed. You need the Medium to work in tandem with the spirit wishing to show. That spirit needs to link with the Medium, and they also need to have built a supply of energy with which they can work. They can use this energy, plus the water in the air and breaths of those sitting, to build a representation of the image that is imprinted into the energy. This image is then shown. There is much said about this practice, but it is harmless for those watching and for the Medium on which the imprint is laid upon.

Qn: Do you use safer energy now? Because I understand that many years ago spirit used something called ectoplasm, is that correct? (Yes). *What is the difference between these two energies being used?*
Chief: One is safe in air mode. The other is a manifestation of the Medium's own energy, so if interrupted by adverse circumstances, the energy returns home too quickly, intensely causing burning of the Medium's body, so not desirable and not safety first.

Qn: Focusing on the safe energy method, is the energy that is generated exterior to the Medium? (Yes). *When spirits show themselves in that energy, does that spirit merge with the Medium?* (No). *Is it an entirely exterior process for the spirit to present in the energy that has been created around a Medium.* (Yes). *Do the Medium's spirit Guides monitor what is happening?*
Chief: Yes always. Who and when, and to watch what the energy level at that time is.

Qn: Is it safe for a person who is watching to put their hand in that energy field?
Chief: It would most probably just disperse. But if that person is another Medium then they could hi-jack the demonstration. You know that from the past and have touched[2].

---

2   There were occasions when members of the Circle were invited to feel the energy being created by spirits during demonstrations. The

Qn: Is physical energy used for transfigurations. (Yes). *What is the difference between the Medium who can achieve a deep trance state and the use of physical energy to move objects.*
Chief: Different sensitivities. One has a more mentor connection, their third eye so to speak is more open and connected to spirit.

Qn: What is the spiritual difference between someone working with physical energy and someone who can enter a deep trance state.
Chief: Third eye[3] is more open in Medium using deep trance state. With physical energy you are physically connected to your Guides, the body transfers physical energy easily. The main Medium here is a jack of all trades, but not of all masters.

Qn: Is part of it a mental attribute? (Yes). *And training?* (Openness).

Communication – Spirit through a Medium (Deep Trance)

Qn: Can you tell us how a spirit communicates directly through a Medium?
Chief: The spirit is using an area of the physical body not always used. It means that there is plenty of space for blending. The human brain does not get used efficiently, and there is plenty of excess capacity.

Qn: Where does the spirit or energy of the Medium go to when they are in a deep trance state?
Chief: It doesn't go anywhere. It steps back into a created place to

---

sensations have often been described as mild tingling sensations in the hand and/or arm when a volunteer placed their hand into the energy field that had been generated by spirits.

3   A third eye is that which provides perception beyond ordinary sight.

rest assured only when the Medium has attained the deep trance state.

Qn: Is there anything else that you would add about what happens when a Medium goes into a deep trance state?
Chief: It means the Medium has entered the state before sleep. It means the Medium is open for us to communicate through them, but the Medium's Guides and Guardian must also be willing to allow this to occur. As you are aware, the spirit often wanders during sleep, but the Guardian sits in and protects. Well, if you can imagine, in a pre-sleep state the Medium is still present and so are their Guides and the Guardian, so this enables a merging of facilities[4], shall we say, so that speech and movement can be obtained.

Qn: Do you distract the Medium's mind? (Yes). *I often find with me that you distract my mind away.*
Chief: So that it is occupied.

Qn: If the visiting spirit who is talking stays too long, can the Medium's own energy displace that visiting spirit? (Yes). *Can you say a little more about what happens?*
Chief: I am feeling that my voice needs to travel further afield, so I will concentrate my energy and focus my thoughts and send them as energy brain waves. You can see these waves on monitors that check activity in the brain. It is shown as electrical bursts of energy.

Qn: Are you saying that the energy waves you speak of are like the waves that our brain uses.
Chief: Yes. Like an electrical energy.

---

4   Merging of facilities is an attempt to describe another spirit merging with the part of the physical body vacated by the Medium, always providing this is allowed by the Medium and their spirit Guardian.

Qn: So, energy can be movement, vibration, electrical, sound ...
Chief: How did that statement grab you?

Qn: Well, I don't know anything about that! But I did EG for people who suffered fits to monitor changes in the brain and whether the waveform was back down. Does that mean by using this equipment we could pick up your communication with our brains if we had that machine on. (Yes). And the medical profession wouldn't have seen it as spirit communication?
Chief: No. Also, you are not really in the meditative state at the point of measurement.

Communication – Spirit to Mediums (Visuals)

Qn: How is it that you can implant those visions that I see.
Chief: The ideas and visions are implanted by using your sensory awareness. It means we can imprint ideas and diagrams into the area of your brain that is usually left dormant. It means you see it separately from your optical vision. We can separate these visions and apply them; even when you are looking at the world with your eyes, we can still give you images to work with.

Qn: Is it a spirit that is giving me images that may be linked to a physical person for me to pass on.
Chief: Yes. This is all controlled within your Aura[5]. You can expand and contract the area allowed for communication.

Qn: How do we see images when the eyes are closed?
Chief: It is us letting you use again the bottom of the eye and

---

5   We all have an aura. This is a form of emanation surrounding the physical body that cannot be seen by the naked eye but is often described as your outer energy field and an integral part of your spirit.

manipulating your third eye or your connections to the body of spirit and allowing you to see what you would not normally see.

Qn: Is this something that you do, or do we do it ourselves is?
Chief: It is cooperation, instigated by you in cooperation with us.

Qn: In doing that, do you come into my aura to be able to do that? (Yes). So, I am allowing you to come in. (Yes). and that's how the two work together by using the third eye? (Yes).

Qn: Then how do you expand the area of the Aura?
Chief: By allowing the Light to come down and for it to surround you in a comfortable protecting way. Then you can focus on your aura, pushing it out gently and allowing those that wish to communicate to enter this region, and they can, using the energy, they can communicate. Your Guides must be told to protect you first. As you develop, you will find that more and more spirits will come.

Communication – Spirit to Medium/Spirit

Qn: How do spirits communicate in the spirit world?
Conglomerate: I am here to speak to you about the art of communication. I can see that you all have a desire to communicate one way or another. You, to your higher being. You, to those loved ones dear departed. You[6], to the crystal users in the past who can help you unlock the way the crystals work and communicate beyond your world. I know that you would like to understand better how this works.

---

6   The Conglomerate was specifically addressing three members of the Circle who wanted to know more about their own communication skills as spiritual Mediums.

To talk of the way that a spirit communicates, it is via vibration but requires no audible sound to be sent through the air, rather it is sound that is almost telepathy. The energy vibrates in such a way to cause like the wind puffs on your hand or cheek[7]. It cannot be seen as it travels to your hand or another's cheek, but it can be felt on arrival. This is the way sound is communicated, you pick up the puff of wind shall we say, and you translate it into sound in your head. The answer to noisy parties[8].

Qn: Are you an expert in communication? (Yes). *How do you communicate, spirit to spirit that is?*
Conglomerate: The same way.

Qn: When spirits come down to talk to us. How do they hear us? Do spirits hear us all the time? Are they subjected to a continual babble in the background? We cannot hear sounds that are higher frequency. Because spirits vibrate higher, do they only hear sounds that are higher?
Conglomerate: I hear only mind sounds in spirit. They are waves generated by your spirit's energy. They give sounds to your energy, and you receive them like talking to one another. The distance has limitations, so you are not bombarded. They are also directional, you can send a request directional over distance, but you can only send them to a single recipient. You cannot pick up human chatter unless you come down to the physical and slow your vibration enough to pick up sense from the waves of sound.

---

7   The Conglomerate is trying to explain what it feels like to receive communication in spirit, i.e. the wind blowing gently on your cheek. He is describing the vibration that is felt by one spirit when another has initiated conversation.

8   This is an amusing reference to partying without making sounds! It shows that spirits also have a sense of humour, and Circle members have had many lighthearted moments during sittings. I understand that silent discos do occur via the use of music played through headphones.

During the same Circle sitting, another spirit visitor came through to speak a few minutes later. This occurrence seemed to provide an opportunity for spirit to demonstrate their capacity to communicate among themselves across significant distances in the spirit world within short periods of time.

Qn: Can you introduce yourself and tell us your name please?
Visitor: Yes, Claire.

Qn: Where are you from? (Australia). Are you of Aborigine culture? (No). Where in Australia?
Claire: Near Darwin.

Qn: Did you live there all your life? (Yes). Were you born in Australia? (Yes). Were your parents born in Australia? (No). Did they emigrate from England?
Claire: Yes, hence, my English name.

Qn: Why are you here?
Claire: To show you that spirit can travel across the globe, without problem. How may you ask? I am given a place to think about that I would like to visit and here I am.

Qn: This is very unusual. Could you tell me how you travelled here from Australia?
Claire: Energy lines.

Qn: Can you be more specific because it's a long way between Australia and England and there was only a pause of less than 10 minutes.

Claire: Not in the grand scheme of things[9].

Qn: Were you asked to come here? (Yes). *So, you were in Australia a little while ago.*
Claire: No, I am in spirit.

Qn: How did you know when to come here?
Claire: It is like having a mobile phone in your head.

Qn: So, you received a message from one of our spirit Guides? (No). *What happened?*
Claire: You asked a question. They sent me to speak to you.

Qn: My question was about communication spirit to spirit. So how did they communicate with you and how did you communicate back with them to say – I'm on my way!
Claire: Easy, it's like having a built-in receiver and microphone. The message travels through energy levels to spirit in Australia, and that distance is not a hindrance.

Qn: Thank you. A simple way to demonstrate, whereas I thought ...
Claire: You do not see the sound waves, do you? The sound waves are vibrations that are caused by our body[10] vibrating in a certain way.

---

9   I do not think that Claire had sufficient knowledge to give all the answers I hoped for, and this maybe highlights that some spirits are accepting, just as we are in the physical world, of existing without questioning. Nevertheless, this was an effective demonstration by spirit of their ability to communicate between themselves over vast distances and travel at speeds we cannot understand.

10   The spirit body is referred to as being of energy and vibration. We tend to associate the human body with our own physical shape, while the body of a spirit may well be an orb, or shapeless, or a form held in the shape of any spirits favoured past life they may have had in the physical world. But it is still a body in both our understandings.

Why do you find it so difficult to understand that energy[11] can also vibrate and then send out the energy equivalent of sound waves that are obviously of a much higher vibration, and which is out of earshot of human hearing.

୭

Although Claire had been able to articulate to the Circle how she engaged in communication and travel within the spirit world at speeds that are incomprehensible, her arrival did provide a basic demonstration of the apparent ease with which spirits were able to use a form of spiritual telepathy for communication and also to travel in remarkably short periods of time, being facilitated by the energy of the Universe. Further details on this subject will be covered in subsequent sections. Claire's visit was brief, and a few minutes later the session was concluded by CP. Before closing, CP offered an additional explanation regarding the methods through which spirits communicate with each other.

Qn: CP, if a spirit in England wanted to talk with a spirit in America, how would they initiate it?
CP: I would just think of them and visualise them. I would think of their spirit's name, like the one that I was originally designated from the beginning.

Qn: I know that you will not tell me the name you were originally designated, but if you did disclose it would I understand it?
CP: Yes, because you know me in the spirit world. We all have

---

11 Claire is referring to her energy (her spirit) vibrating in a certain manner that make the sound waves enabling conversation with other spirits.

unusual names in spirit, otherwise how would I know you with all the names that you have[12].

Qn: Does your message travel distances through energy lines?
CP: Yes, and energy lines cross through all the spirit world and over great distances.

Communication – Using Physical Objects

Having addressed the ability of mental mediumship, there is an alternative method of communication that is unique and often disregarded due to its dependence on the use of physical energy. In the first instance, it is important to conduct all communication with spirits within a safe environment, especially when physical energy is being used for such purposes. This method involves spirits utilising physical energy to move physical objects. Let me be quite clear, our Circle has never used a Ouija Board and nor do the spirits we engage with endorse the use of such a medium for communication either. The Ouija Board functions similarly to an antenna for any spirit passing by and can be a hazardous method, potentially attracting troublesome earthbound spirits that may attach themselves to users.

I decided to acquire a small wooden tri-leg circular table to explore whether spirits could move it using the physical energy they might be able to generate. For six months Rita and I conducted private weekly one-hourly sittings, during which we

---

12   CP is referring to the many lives and names that we will all have acquired as we transition between many physical and spirit existences. There are spirits that have known and worked with each other over long periods of time who revert to using the name that they will have been allocated with at 'birth', a spiritual name or ID by which they are recognised in the spirit world. Thus, everyone will have a singular name in spirit that will differ from the names they may have acquired throughout their many lives in the physical.

sat across the table from each other with hands placed lightly on the table in a dimly lit room. It took immense patience and dedication, and we came very close to abandoning our efforts when success was finally achieved, the table tipped sideways when we were least expecting it to. From that point onwards, we had weekly 'table tipping sessions' where movement of the table became more fluid.

Eventually, spirits were able to harness the physical energy generated to move various objects placed on the table and also developed an ability to tip the table sideways a number of times to identify letters of the alphabet, thereby forming words and sentences. Although initially a slow and laborious process, this method of communication proved to be an effective way for spirits to convey their messages without requiring a Medium to enter a trance state. Furthermore, it ensured that all participants were fully engaged with the messages being delivered.

Progress did not remain static for long. The spirit Guides became highly proficient at delivering their messages by moving a small circular drum around the table surface to give their messages as handwritten words[13] in cursive script that form coherent sentences. Witnessing the varied handwriting styles of different spirit visitors was quite awesome to watch and this new practice became a method that was regularly used by spirits for a very large part of the conversational transcripts published in this book.

Qn: You have become very adept at moving this drum around the table to write sentences. How do you move the drum? (Energy). *How do you move physical objects?* (Energy). *How are you moving this drum now?* (Energy). *We have our fingers placed very lightly*

---

13   This incredible breakthrough for us occurred during the time of the COVID restrictions in 2019-20.

on the drum, and we are not moving it, so how... (Energy).

Qn: We can't see you because you're vibrating a lot higher than our vision will allow, but are you somehow touching the drum and pushing it to move it?
Chief: No. We move it by moving the energy around. We envelop the drum in energy, and by making more on certain sides it creates movement[14].

Qn: Does it take one of you to do that?
Chief: No. There needs to be a number to create the energy and movement.

Qn: Does daylight affect what you do? (Yes). *Should we keep the drum and table in darkness when we are not sitting?*
Chief: Yes. Light is made up of many frequencies and they all affect the frequencies of the table and drum energy that we use.

Qn: Does daylight weaken your energy?
Chief: No, it is dispersed, and we are always changing the vibration.

Qn: If we did not have our fingers placed on the drum, would you still be able to move it?
Chief: What would be the point?

Qn: You might want to frighten someone! (No). *Understood, but there might be a spirit who wants to show a loved one that they are still around, is that permissible?*
Chief: Yes. Also, wafts of scent, thoughts of the past, and pictures of what has been come to mind.

---

14   This is further explored in the Section titled 'Energy and Bumps and Bangs'.

Qn: How do you create physical energy to move objects.
Chief: It builds from around the area where you sit.

Qn: Do you use thought processes as well?
Chief: Yes always. We are only human.

Qn: Sorry, could you clarify that please.
Chief: We are all spirits that have lived in the physical before, so all are human in your eyes. Just a label for conversation.

~

The response provided by the Chief to the penultimate question was particularly impactful for our Circle – 'we are only human' – emphasising that we are the same and we originate from energy. In future interactions with spirits, it may be more appropriate and respectful to refer to them as Soul Persons or Soul People. This terminology also acknowledges the essence of our shared nature, which is later described in this book as only being distinguished by varying ranges of vibrations.

Occasionally, visiting spirits were permitted to evaluate the advancements in our communication methods. Here is what one such spirit visitor had to say about it.

Qn: You are a new visitor, why are you here?
Visitor: I am here to experience the whole physical movement of the drum. I am sure that you will see that I am quite accomplished at this. I am enjoying the ability to communicate so freely and quickly. I feel it is quite freeing and not dependent on someone translating my words and often changing them as they cannot listen to a full conversation like I can have with you now.

Qn: Have you been to the Light? (Yes). *And are you now enjoying the freedom to pop backwards and forwards?* (Yes). *You've obviously tried to get messages across in the past.* (Yes). *Have you been trying to go through trance mediums?* (No). *I'm glad you enjoyed the experience.*

Crystals

Qn: You have told us that a crystal will retain energy. (Yes). *What purpose are crystals used for?*
Chief: They hold and retain different energy and vibrations; this allows work and healing, for example, to be given by certain crystals for certain aims, depending on need. But the energy is not endless, and a crystal should be recharged in sunlight or moonlight regularly if in use, otherwise they may start to drain rather than to give.

Qn: Is that because the crystal holds the energy that it is made from. (Yes). *Is the energy of a crystal the same in both spirit and physical world?* (Yes). *Does it look the same?*
Chief: Yes. Why would it choose not to.

Qn: Thought you would have more energy in the spirit world.
Chief: They come with enough energy from their formation.

Based on the above-mentioned conversation, it seems that it is advisable to position crystals in a location where they can be recharged by exposure to sunlight or moonlight. Crystals are primarily used for healing purposes and personal wellbeing. Furthermore, crystals seem capable of accumulating and storing energy for use by spirits in various activities. Their role in communication appears to function as an energy storage medium rather than as a communication device.

It is evident that spirits employ various types of energy beyond communication for other purposes, including demonstrations through Mediums, healing, and the movement of physical objects. Although I cannot provide a detailed explanation of these distinctions, it is evident that spirits prepare thoroughly for each type of activity they undertake. They always seemed to be able to consistently ensure thorough advance preparation for the specific type of Circle sitting being conducted.

Guides, Spirits (and IDs)

The identity and role of some of the spirits who frequently engaged with the Circle are introduced in this Section.

It is widely acknowledged that every individual in the physical has spirit Guides that accompany them throughout a physical life. For those new to this concept, most individuals will have at least three spirit Guides who provide support throughout their lifetime. There are exceptions where individuals are undertaking special tasks or are advancing spiritually at a rate that influences their spiritual vibration. Such individuals are likely to have larger teams of spirits Guides or may experience mid-term changes to their Guide team to reflect their progression.

The transcripts of the conversations in this book have been facilitated by the cooperation of spirit Guides, who managed the Circle from their side and contributed valuable insights into the spirit world during each meeting. Apart from ensuring the availability of a peaceful environment to work with spirit and transcribing the recordings of the conversations, there was very little else for me to do.

In this Section spirit discusses with us the functions of a spirit Guide, some of the processes involved by which a spirit becomes a Guide, and whether there is a natural spiritual form distinct from the human physical form. I also ask several of the regular spirit visitors, who have collaborated with us for many years and continue to do so, to introduce themselves and share their personal knowledge and experiences regarding the afterlife. Some spirits exhibit a willingness to disclose information about themselves, offering some insights into their personalities, others remain guarded and only willing to provide minimal information.

The Chief

The Chief introduced himself as being responsible for overseeing and supervising the safe operation of the Circle from their side of the spiritual realm when physical energy is utilised. His chosen name for us to recognise him by reflects his American First Nation heritage. The Chief is not specifically assigned as a spirit Guide to any individual associated with the Circle but is always on hand to open sittings where physical energy is used. He has made many telling contributions to this publication.

Qn: Can you tell us about your role with this Circle.
Chief: I am here to watch over this Circle, as you are fully aware. My days have been in the training of others in this field. You find it requires a different skillset to being a Guide for it involves management of others, the ability to problem solve, and to lead in a safe direction. Also, I am needed for protection and the organisation of those that would come before you for communication, demonstration and for the help needed to relocate[15] into the Light.

Qn: Please tell me what you are, and your form.
Chief: I am the energy of myself. It has grown and evolved through experience. We all start as an unwritten slate, a pure energy with a very basic amount of programming. Then as we evolve our vibration changes, it lifts and increases.

---

15   This is covered in more detail under the Sections dealing with 'Earthbound Spirits' and 'The Light'.

Qn: Are you translucent. (No). *Can you describe your colours?*
Chief: I am the colour of light.

Qn: In your natural form, how do you look?
Chief: As a bright light. A ball of pure energy.

Qn: Is that different to an Orb? (No). *Can you appear as an Orb or ball of pure light energy?* (Yes). *So, when we can't see you, is it because you are small or translucent?*
Chief: No. I vibrate out of your vision. Think of the early Teacher's[16] visits, the Medium's hand was a demonstration of this.

Qn: Is any Spirit different to this?
Chief: Yes, it depends on your Level.

Qn: What do you do?
Chief: Apart from this Circle, when you go away or do not sit for other reasons, others guard this room, and I return home and see my family and friends.

Qn: In what dimension do you exist for your home?
Chief: Level eight.

Qn: Are you allowed into nine? (No). *What must you do to get there?* (Progress). *How would you progress?*
Chief: By the work I do here.

Qn: Is your light coloured?

---

16 A reference to the earlier visits from the Conglomerate (Teacher) to discuss the Source which you can read about in the Section titled 'The Source and the Spirit World'. There was a six-year lapse in time between what the Chief has said, and the events that are referred to.

Chief: Yes, gold.

Qn: If you're gold, will you stay that way?
Chief: I hope so.

Qn: What do you mean? What can happen?
Chief: I don't know. But some return to Earth and have a bit of their shine knocked off[17].

Qn: Is there a need for all spirits to come down to the physical.
Chief: No. But sometimes you need to get rid of karma[18].

The Conglomerate (Teacher)

The Teacher is a spirit entity who identifies as a Conglomerate, described as a collection of multiple spirit minds. Initially, the Conglomerate visited the Circle a few times when utilising the deep trance state attained by the Medium to answer questions about the Source. The Conglomerate usually visited to provide clarity of responses to more complex subjects.

Qn: Would you tell me about yourself?
Teacher: I am many, and I come as myself with others[19].

---

17   He is referring to those spirts that come down to the physical world and may not achieve their chosen path or do worse in the physical than might have been planned for. It, perhaps, alludes to all spirits being at risk of returning to the spirit realm at a lower vibration than they may have previously held.

18   Karma is the guilt or regret carried by spirits from their physical life when returning to the spirit realm. It has nothing to do with human physical disability and is briefly addressed in the Section titled 'Karma'.

19   It was only after several visits by the Teacher that we came to realise the Teacher was a spirit entity and visiting from a spirit collective. Whereas the Teacher often arrived as a Conglomerate, the Teacher spoke through the Medium as an individual.

Qn: *Are you a representative or messenger of the Creator?*
Teacher: That is a very good question, my friend. Let us just say, I am a Conglomerate.

Qn: *We have heard that description used before.*
Conglomerate: Made of a few and made of many.

Qn: *Are you defined as a messenger?*
Conglomerate: I am defined as a teacher. I am here to teach.

Qn: *Are you an angel?*
Conglomerate: I am beyond that. Let us put it this way, we are not one of the prophets, but we do our best to supply knowledge.

Qn: *Can you describe the Conglomerate.*
Conglomerate: A group of like-minded spirits that have bonded together.

Qn: *Where do you reside in Spirit?*
Conglomerate: Where we choose to operate, for us we have a library. We are the keepers of books. Every book written by mankind is in that library. Plus, copies of some of the books that are yet to be written.

Qn: *What qualification do you need to join the Conglomerate.*
Conglomerate: Our love and passion for what we stand for and do. That is knowledge, books, invention, technology, history. Those are my personal preferences.

Qn: *Tell me more about the Conglomerate.*
Conglomerate: The Conglomerate is made up of those that have a likened image. A likened… how can I describe it to you… A likened passion… a likened passion for a similar outlook upon life, so spirits

come together to share that outlook on life. They blend into one and become a Conglomerate, and as they join the Conglomerate, they bring all the knowledge that they have into the Conglomerate. It becomes one very large energy of knowledge.

Qn: Are there other Conglomerates?
Conglomerate: Many. All with lots of different things, and ours is one of learning, books. The love of mankind's knowledge. There are others that like to focus upon music, the arts of mankind, for that has gone through your entire existence, and it has brought together generations with those that have a similar talent.

Qn: As an individual, what do you like?
Conglomerate: What do I like? I like knowledge. Knowledge to me is like food and drink, though we do not need to consume food or drink. When you return home to spirit, you are energy. That energy is all you need and comes from the love of the Creator and the Light in which you dwell. The food and drink for me is knowledge.

Qn: And what are your interests?
Conglomerate: Investigating knowledge, gaining knowledge, learning what is going to happen. It is a passion for me. In my time on the Earth, I was always interested in the investigation of things. It is a passion within you that knows no bounds. I am here because I am bringing my passion to you.

Spirit Guides

Qn: Do spirits preparing for physical re-birth to Earth select their own Guides?
Chief: Select before born to physical Earth. You may choose half, and Source/Council in great halls may choose half. When you choose, you may invite friends or family best suited to help you.

Qn: How are Guides appointed?
Chief: It depends. A spirit can apply, or voice their interest, or be part of a long-term friendship group. Then all is considered to increase your capabilities in achieving your set goals. It is no good giving a world-famous violinist a champion sprinter or hockey player, for example, they may not understand the delicate path you are about to embark on. But saying that, they will understand dedication and hard work.

Qn: How do the Council select the Guides of their choice?
Conglomerate: It comes down to what the individual wishes to achieve from their physical lifespan as they obviously would need help in the direction of their intended path. You may pick people that you have been attached to, mixed with family and you may pick these people to accompany your little group, but it is no good if none of them are specialised within the field that you wish to undertake this time[20]. So, it is better to have a more balanced view. You will have half that you pick yourself and half that have been given to you with the intention of helping you specifically through your path. They will look at your plan and look at who is available at that time, then call them and offer them this position. They may take it, they may not. It is their prerogative. They would read the circumstances and decide that they can comfortably manage it, or they may decide that they are not up to what they can see as the chaos within the human facility.

Qn: Did I choose four close friends from spirit family? (Yes). *Were they successful in the selection?* (Yes). *You say four. That is Teacher, Healer, Guardian, and who is the fourth?*

---

20 The Conglomerate refers to the new physical existence that an individual is set to embark upon after experiencing numerous past lives in the physical world.

Chief: No, you cannot pick Guardian or Lead Guide.[21] Conflict of interest.

Qn: So, who is the fourth Guide?
Chief: Lead Guide.

Qn: What is the difference between a Guardian Angel and a Guide?
Chief: Your Guardian is really the most important Guide, or if you prefer Angels, their job is to protect your physical body when you[22] choose to walk about when asleep and to protect you all the time as well. Their job is likened to your presidential bodyguard.

Guardian Guide

Qn: Welcome Fritz, have you been a Guide to many people? (Yes). So, you are an experienced Guide. (Yes). What is your specialism? (Guardian).[23] What did it take for you to become a Guide?
Fritz: I had to show an interest.

Qn: What process did you go through to become a Guide?
Fritz: I had an interview, then an adaptation process.

Qn: Who selected you?
Fritz: The Council.

---

21   This suggests the two Guides you may select can be your Teacher and Healer, not your Guardian or Lead Guide who are selected by a spirit Council. Of course, you may have more than four Guides in the Team, and this suggests that you may also be allowed to select friends or family as Guides who will not have a specific role to play.
22   This is referring to when you, in your spiritual energy form, may decide to leave your physical body and go walkabout.
23   One of two guardian Guides assigned to a Medium.

*Qn: Who are the Council? (*Councillors*). What is their role? (*No response*)*[24]*. What specialisms do you need to become a Guide?*
Fritz: Experience of people. Preferably of Life.

*Qn: Did you know your Charge in spirit before you became their Guide? (*Yes*). Did you join your Charge immediately prior to their physical birth? (*Yes*). What was your role? (*Guardian*). Were you able to communicate with your Charge prior to their birth? (*Yes*). And have you been their Guardian ever since? (*Yes*). In your role as Guardian, what do you do?*
Fritz: I watch over her and I am with my partner[25] watching over her twenty-four seven, and it is to protect her spirit door, so to speak.

*Qn: So, if you share the job is it easier for you? (*Yes*). Does having two Guardians allow one to have time to see their own family? (*Yes*). And with this arrangement, you decide amongst yourselves? (*No response*). Is it designated? (*Yes*). I suppose that saves arguments. (*Yes*).*

*Qn: Do you ever have to attend re-training? (*Yes*). What would that be for?*
Fritz: To learn to keep up with her development.

*Qn: Do you have to re-train to keep up with development? (*Yes*). What might that be for?*
Fritz: Communication. Also, the raising of vibration.

Teacher Guide

Qn: Welcome. Are you here to speak with us?

---

24   This question had already been answered by the Conglomerate and Chief.

25   Fritz is referring another Guardian with whom he is sharing responsibility, owing to the spiritual work that is being undertaken.

Cassandra: I am the Teacher Guide you requested. My name is Cassandra. I have been a teacher many times to many Charges. Now, I am learning all the time as well due to the ever-changing world experience that we find our Charges are facing, and I am there to try and guide the Charge through their lives by teaching them, if possible, by nudges, the right approach, and way to go.

Qn: Cassandra, thank you for coming in to talk to us. Can you say who you are Guide for?
Cassandra: One of you here.

Qn: Will you say who? (No). Have you been with your Charge since their birth? (Yes). Are you part of a group of spirits or were you appointed by the Council? (Appointed). Obviously if you cannot directly communicate with your Charge, how can you point them in the right direction?
Cassandra: It is the way they need to walk to achieve their goals or purpose.

Qn: I think you are saying it's not about teaching history or geology. (No). Is it about teaching them how to go about their life.
Cassandra: No. They have free will. I teach them, by nudges, the direction they need to take to achieve their goals and wishes, and they can then return home[26] achieving what they tasked themselves with.

Qn: When do you talk to your Charge, when they are asleep?
Cassandra: It depends.

Qn: Can you talk to your Charge's higher consciousness?
Cassandra: Yes, and with dreams and those feelings that 'this is best'.

---

26   Spirits often referred to the spirit world as home.

Although you don't know why, the same goes for when you feel something is not right or it is wrong.

Qn: Thank you. Cassandra, have you lived in the physical world? (Yes). *Would you be willing to share with us a past life that you have had.* (No). *Thank you for talking about the teaching that you do.*

Healer Guide

A third member of an individual's Guide team is the Healing Guide. It was with some surprise that Harry Edwards (a renowned Healer) visited the Circle to speak on the responsibilities of the Healing Guide. Although not a Guide, Harry became a regular visitor to the monthly distance Healing Circles.

Qn: Good evening. Who is visiting?
Visitor: Harry Edwards.

Qn: Welcome Harry. I thought it would be a healing Guide who would be talking with us.
Harry: What do you think I do. I help and work with the Guides and guide them.

Qn: Sorry I did not mean it that way. Is the healing Guide assigned to look after the physical body or the spirit?
Harry: Both, but mainly spirit. The Guide uses and controls the energy for healing, where it goes, and to who and for what and when.

Qn: I know when my physical body is ill, but I am unaware if my spirit becomes shallow. Will my healer Guide be aware?
Harry: The Guide will be fully aware of the state of your spiritual and physical self.

Qn: Can you tell us about the role of a healing Guide. What do they do, what do they look after and how? There may be people who have terminal illnesses that cannot be healed and might feel disappointment they have not been.

Harry: Ah. Now, there's a question. They heal. But you must remember it could be that person's path. Many forget they can sit for their own healing as well as helping others. You can get your Guide to heal you or if that is not on the cards to help ease your suffering, as you would ask your healer Guide to help others that come to you for healing. It is a case of being the spiritual doctor's assistant.

Qn: Let's say that I have an illness, metaphorically speaking. What might my healing Guide be doing and what energy would they be using?

Harry: The Guide would use the appropriate level of energy for the task ahead. For example, if you were to help someone with cancer you would not want to speed up the cell repair or production, if you did that it would be inappropriate. If it was, for example, medical stress related to the mind, you would need to be very gentle in the mind and use a different level and vibration to align the aura and body energy, it is again a different energy level and vibration. You could say type of.

Qn: Can my Spirit become ill or shallow and what happens if it does? Am I making sense?

Harry: Yes. Your Spirit does not become ill in the same sense as your physical. But it is linked to every part of your physical body so it will feel everything although it does not actually hurt in the same way. It can get out of sorts with it not realising that it feels emotions more and so can become out of sorts, depressed, etc. This can be the job of a healer Guide to help, and this can help regain an inner peace and a bolster of acceptance in the situation that has caused this. A healer Guide will help and support them through physical problems as well as the effects on their Spirit.

Qn: When I put my hand out to help somebody, how does the healing Guide work, what does the Guide do?
Harry: The Guide will gather the appropriate energy and fine tune it, then send it down the outside of your arm to your hand. The energy is then radiated from your hand into the physical person's energy that you are giving healing to and will, with the aid and assistance of that person's own healer Guide, direct it to the right spot to start its appropriate work.

Qn: Thank you. Changing the subject a little, do you hop in and out of the Light?
Harry: Yes. But I bring the Light with me.

Qn: And when you return to the Light, where do you go?
Harry: My home is where my family is.

Qn: You spend a lot of time doing healing, do you have time for doing other things in your life?
Harry: There is an eternity.

Qn: If your favourite thing is healing, what is your second favourite thing?
Harry: Reading and enjoying the company of my family.

Lead Guide

Qn: Can you tell us who you are please?
Lead Guide: I am with S.... My work entails keeping order amongst the team of Guides. I work collectively on many projects within the field of her exploration of this world and its place in her universe. We look forward and backward from this point and all points to anticipate as best we can pass through the ups and downs that create the aims of life. I keep a close eye on the functioning of the individual

members of her team of Guides to ensure that their duties are carried out to perfection as best they can.

Qn: Were you appointed? (Yes). *Who appointed you?*
Lead Guide: All is decided before you even come down to this Earth plane.

Qn: Did you have to undergo an interview or apply? What happened?
Lead Guide: I was vetted and had to undergo an interview. I knew S…, as she is now called, before she decided to make this journey to this place. Any karma and replace it with all the love she has and is capable of, to the forefront of her life.

Qn: What sort of experience did you have personally to become a Lead Guide.
Lead Guide: I have been all but a healer in my time. I have done some healing but it not my strongest suit. I have worked my way up the ladder to achieve this position. This time is my third as a Lead Guide.

S…: *I would love to know your name please.*
Lead Guide: You may refer to me as Emmanuel.

Apprentice Guide

We can all be forgiven for assuming that spirit Guides are experienced but like in the physical world everyone has to start somewhere. Some spirit Guides may be new or relatively inexperienced or just embarking on a new career in their spirit realm and learning their trade. We were fortunate to be engaging in the following discussion with an apprentice Guide who had taken up a first tour of duty within my spirit Guide team.

Qn: Welcome Alicia. I know from our previous conversations that you initially missed the Light and had crossed over late. (Yes). When did you decide after going into the Light that you wanted to become a Guide?
Alicia: I decided before I went into the Light that I would like to be a Guide like those in your and the Medium's Guide teams.

Qn: Do you have to go into the Light first before you can become an apprentice Guide.
Alicia: I do not know the answer to that.

Qn: Alicia, could you ask one of your colleagues the answer to the question you could not answer please.
Alicia: You can come from the Light as a special Guide. You must have been in the Light first.

Qn: What process did you have to go through to become an apprentice Guide?
Alicia: They asked me lots of questions, then showed me people in certain situations and asked me how I would react and what I felt I should do.

Qn: Are you training for a particular Guide specialism?
Alicia: Not at the moment. I have to become an experienced Guide first.

Qn: Who was it that asked you those questions or interviewed you?
Alicia: A very kind lady from a Council.

Qn: When you were successful did you choose where you wished to go?
Alicia: To the kind couple that helped me[27].

---

27 Alicia is referring to her rescue several years after her own passing from physical into spirit.

Qn: Could you describe some of the training that you do?
Alicia: They test me every now and then about how I was, and how I felt I was doing, was I happy, and did I feel I needed more assistance from the Council members.

Qn: For you to become a full Guide, what is it you achieve or do?
Alicia: You must fulfil their criteria and have gained enough experience in the field and be able to answer their questions. Then you get a naming ceremony with a special badge of honour.

Qn: At the end of the apprenticeship is there an official ceremony, like students passing their exams will have?
Alicia: Yes, but not for many years.[28]

Qn: Do you have to serve with others as an apprentice Guide before you can become a full Guide?
Alicia: I do not know. I just must experience all of a human's life span and then a lot of their issues and problems.

Qn: Does it depend how well you are doing at the end of this apprenticeship, then the Council will decide?
Alicia: Not this time. I joined you later in life. I need to experience from birth, etc.

Qn: Alicia, we know that you are a wonderful ballet dancer, but would you tell us about one of your other past lives in the physical world?
Alicia: I was around as a main servant in the 17th century. It was hard work.

---

28   Alicia is referring to her Guide apprenticeship taking a while.

Qn: Were you a servant to an individual?
Alicia: Yes, I looked after the Mistress. I did not do the housework. I did pressing, stitching, dressing, serving, etc.

Qn: That's very descriptive and much appreciated. Did you marry?
Alicia: No, once you did you were terminated in your employment in the House.

Qn: Where was this?
Alicia: England and India. We also travelled in Europe.

Qn: Did the people that you worked for have high status.
Alicia: Wealthy. Importing and exporting. Not slaves.

Qn: When you get moments in spirit with little to do, what do you do?
Alicia: Time, history, dance, anything I fancy doing, and meeting of minds with groups of people

Qn: Who do you mix with most?
Alicia: These groups who are in the room with us.

Qn: What is your favourite art?
Alicia: Dance. Favourite is Sibelius.

Qn: How do you like to appear yourself?
Alicia: As for myself, I wear all my best designed clothes from the 1930s. It is more feminine.

Names and IDs

Getting on first name terms with someone can help put others at ease, and a name given by a spirit is typically the name they prefer to be recognised by when they visit. In some instances, the name chosen by a spirit may be one that they had been known by during a previous physical life, or it could be another preferred name or title. Whatever name they use will be familiar to you and not necessarily the name they are known by with other spirits. This step is crucial towards understanding how spirits attempt to normalise their interaction with humans, when considering the different personas a spirit can take; it is perfectly acceptable for an individual spirit to have had a number of physical incarnations while still maintaining their singular presence in the spirit realm.

Qn: Can we discuss the logistics of Spirit interaction in the physical?
Chief: I will talk about circles and infinity signs.

Qn: Go ahead.
Chief: The circle is one half for infinity. No matter how many times or not you cross the circle you always end up back at the start. Your home.

Qn: Is this an example of something? (Metaphor). *Are you referring to going backwards and forwards between spirit and physical.*
Chief: Yes. Life exists in both places. It exists for you in both worlds. The difference is that in the physical world your circumstances evolve with each visit.

Qn: What happens when you return to Spirit?
Chief: You are a core. That is what defines you, the rest is just a persona. The knowledge learnt and experience gained is in your original self.

Qn: Trying to put this in perspective. Every time a spirit comes to the physical, they will be different. (Yes). *Every time that someone returns to spirit...*

Chief: Wait. Your physical is different; your physical self is intact albeit half accessible to you.

Qn: Are you saying that the core self or spirit is the same through all an individual's reincarnations? (Yes). *Do you take the persona and knowledge of the person you had been in the physical when you return to the spirit world.* (Yes). *After a little while in Spirit, can a person choose any other persona that they may have had in past incarnations in the physical?*
Chief: The personas can only represent them.

Qn: Got it. Our spirit has its own individual ID. (Yes). *That ID is not the persona of who that individual is in spirit.* (Yes). *But each time that a spirit enters a new physical body they will adopt a different persona.* (Yes). *And when they return to spirit, they adopt their original ID.* (Yes). *Because that is how you recognise each other in the spirit world.* (Yes). *That said, a spirit may choose, when conversing with physical people, the persona that they will be recognised as.* (Yes). *In spirit, it is your spirit ID that shows who you really are.* (Yes).

Qn: Is the ID your Soul. (Yes).

As you progress further into this book, you may come to realise there is an intrinsic link between the physical and spiritual worlds reflecting the existence of a never-ending circle of interchanging life.

Section 2

The Source and Spirit World

The Library Circle held discussions with various visiting spirits focusing on the nature of the spirit world, including its mechanisms for existence and sustainability. These discussions naturally led to curiosity about its origins, energy, and self-sustaining characteristics. We were told that all things originate from energy and its Source, and it seemed a good idea to inquire further into the nature of this Source. According to English dictionaries, a Source is defined as anything from which something originates or can be obtained.

Is energy really the Source of where life may have originated from? The physical world we live in encompasses a multitude of faiths, religious beliefs, and cultures, each with their own conclusions about the origins of life. I believe it is best to respect and allow each to continue to draw their own conclusions on this subject, as in these contexts, a Source or God is the ultimate deity to be worshipped. Whether an individual chooses to identify as an atheist, scientist, astronomer, or follower of a specific religious belief, I hope it can be generally recognised that the Universe and all life within it may have originated from the same point of inception. This raises the question about the origins and development of life on Earth or within the Universe since creation.

Scientists seem to generally agree that the universe is composed of matter and energy at the two highest component levels, and beneath these are molecules and other miniscule particles or energies that I do not claim to know anything about and will not delve into to avoid becoming embroiled in a subject that is best left answered by Science and the Cosmos. But within this framework, how and where does spiritual life fit? It does not exist as a life above the clouds or in the heavens, but perhaps it exists within or parallel with physical life here on Earth, unseen by us in another dimension and in what form.

While some members of the Circle sought to explore and understand more about spirits and the afterlife, others were also interested in inquiring about the origins of the Universe and how the spirit world integrated within the broader context of creation and physical existence on Earth. Additionally, given the vastness of the Universe, some questioned whether there are multiple sources of creation, I was aware of this being a complex subject to pursue and I did not know whether the spirits would be receptive to such inquiries.

This Section provides extracts from the transcripts of several conversations with spirits covering questions raised by members of the Circle relating to the Source. The first conversation occurred in 2014 with a spirit who identified as a teacher. The name stuck, and the Teacher became a regular spirit visitor to answer questions about the Source, and other topics related to life in the spirit world. At the time of the Teacher's first visit, it was not known that the Teacher formed part of a spiritual collective known as a Conglomerate[29].

The Teacher usually visited when the Medium had entered a deep trance state. The visits always seemed to coincide with the Medium's right hand shaking to an almost visual blur for the entire duration of her trance state, which often lasted

---

29 A Conglomerate is defined as a collection or number of different and distinct parts that are grouped together. In this case, it is a collection of spiritual knowledge and experience held by this group of individual spirits that came together to form a Conglomerate.

for over one hour. The shaking hand did not appear to cause the Medium any physical discomfort or after effect, though I should add that upon exiting the deep trance state the Medium had no recollection of the conversation that had taken place. Out of concern for the Medium's well-being, I asked why this happened and this was the Teacher's response:

> "I slow down to come on to this Level, but I cannot slow everything down. It is the hand that I am using for illustration, for if I bring the other hand in, you see (*now the other hand is vibrating to a blur*) it vibrates as well."

Initially, the Teacher insisted that the information could not to be published until I had acquired a better understanding of the spirit world as a whole. It was quite a few years before the Conglomerate finally gave permission for most of the answers to be published.

The Source – First conversation (also the first visit)

Qn: Please identify yourself.
Teacher: It is a while since I have done this[30]. I am afraid you do not have Sebastian[31] this evening. For questions on the Source he (Sebastian)[32] has requested a higher information source. So, having heard of the family, I have decided to come this evening. This is

---

30 The Teacher is referring to his use of the deep trance state to speak through a spiritual Medium for this visit.

31 Sebastian had been the previous regular spirit visitor assigned to the teaching sessions the Circle up to this point.

32 It was Sebastian who had previously referred to the Creator or universal energy as the Source.

special and I will answer questions that you have that I may be able to answer or may not be allowed to. We shall see as we progress.

Qn: That's fine.
Teacher: I will attempt to stabilise; I have not done this for a long time. I will stabilise more as time progresses. Now please ask your first question.

Qn: I understand there may be several Sources[33]; Is there more than one source of creation that exists in the Universe?
Teacher: There is one Ultimate Source that controls them all. But there are, shall we say, sons and daughters as a description. Each of these Individual Sources are given their own area to look after, all working with the same love and energy.

Qn: Are these son and daughter Sources classified as our ultimate creator – or is the Ultimate Source the Creator of human life?
Teacher: The single Source is the Ultimate Source. But our Individual Source is referred to by most religions and it is the one in control of our environment but watched at all times by the Ultimate Source.

Qn: Is this Ultimate Source energy based?
Teacher: All is energy based.

Qn: Everything?
Teacher: Everything, even the most solid of objects, has a certain level of energy in it.

Qn: We have been told that spirit can exist on 12 multi-dimensional Levels. If Level 1 is the Ultimate Source, and no one else can reside

---

33   During earlier discussions and teachings Sebastian had referred to there being more than one source of creation in the Universe.

in the energy of the Ultimate Source, do we only reach Level 2 or 3?
Teacher: No, they may be absorbed into Level 1 if that is their true desire, but at that point however they will lose all their own identity and become part of the Ultimate Source, combining their energy into the greater energy.

Qn: What does that mean? What purpose does that serve?
Teacher: For those that choose that path, which is their ultimate goal. For they may have been on the path for a long time striving to reach perfection and striving to attain their ultimate goal. To be absorbed into the Ultimate Source is the ultimate goal.

Qn: Why would they choose to do that?
Teacher: Why does anyone have these desires? It is ideal for some, for the sake of the world, to live only to be working towards perfection.

Qn: Does that mean they will no longer exist as individuals?
Teacher: They lose their identity. So, they become part of... absorbed into if you like... their energy combines with the rest, and they become part of the Ultimate Source.

Qn: Can someone on Level 2 communicate with the Ultimate Source? How would they communicate?
Teacher: The Ultimate Source can communicate with any Level.

Qn: Is the Ultimate Source all seeing?
Teacher: The Ultimate Source is aware of a lot but has eyes in others.

Qn: Does the Ultimate Source allow worlds to carry on as it wishes?
Teacher: It has eyes in others. It is not just the Ultimate Source that keeps watch, others also keep watch. The Ultimate Source has been down to this Level and has communicated with people on this Level but only special people for the Ultimate Source is too strong for most.

The Ultimate Source also has, how should we say, agents within the spirit world that keep an eye out, and should they foresee problems, will consult with the Ultimate Source. It is much like I suspect your hierarchy on this planet still.

Qn: If the Ultimate Source, exists as an energy, is it the highest vibration frequency that exists?
Teacher: It is pure, it is love.

Qn: And if the Ultimate Source wishes to slow down his energy, can that be achieved to communicate with others?
Teacher: The Ultimate Source can do that, but he is very strong, and it does tend to leave a mark, it takes a while to disperse.

Qn: Is this because the energy is significant?
Teacher: That is correct.

Qn: Could it be harmful?
Teacher: No, he would not communicate with anyone who could not take his energy. He would pick someone else to communicate a message to them from him. It comes down to the level that they can understand.

Qn: Is the Ultimate Source the creator of the physical world?
Teacher: The Ultimate Source is the creator of energy, and all comes from energy. There was nothing...

Qn: I am having trouble understanding that one.
Teacher: Energy combines to form substance. I know it is hard for you to grasp. They have been working on it for millennials.

Qn: Just like the big bang theory?
Teacher: Yes, I have heard of that.

Qn: Where did the Ultimate Source come from?
Teacher: That is a question that is beyond your comprehension at this time. It would quite literally blow your mind to understand that. It is a very complex answer, and should I give you all the details of that involved, you would not be able to follow it. Suffice it to say, it is there. The energy that made the Individual Source came from the original Ultimate Source.

Qn: If there are several Individual Sources in the Universe, can spirits travel to another Individual Source area or dimension?
Teacher: You can if that is your wish. To be born within another dimension as you call it, then this can be facilitated. But this cannot be facilitated unless you go through the Ultimate Source itself. Does that answer your question?

Qn: Yes. Is there anything, if you were giving me a lesson on the Source, that you would tell me about the Source that I couldn't possibly have thought of.
Teacher: It is better if you ask the questions, for that means your mind has dwelled on the facts you have been given, and your natural curiosity and understanding is best taken in small doses. For then you take in, you dwell upon, and then you understand that portion; and that portion lets your mind open to more questions and that way your progression is guided through your own understanding rather than me sitting here and just spouting facts at you that have no relevance to your understanding at this point in time. I think to progress this way is to develop a proper understanding of the information at hand.

Qn: Is the Individual Source, directing or controlling progress on the Earth plane?
Teacher: On the Earth plane and sometimes more in the spirit world

in preparation for the Earth plane. For the Individual Source has tried to give all their own choices.

Qn: Does the Individual Source provide for some gifted spirits to come down to the Earth plane to provide certain advancements for the physical plane? If so, how could this happen?
Teacher: Exactly as you say. It is decided that a little bit of something is needed just to give guidance. Whether they take it or not is their choice, but it is there. We have many gifted spirits with lots of knowledge. We do not mind this task. They may not come as one, or they may come as two and three destined to meet and work together if all progresses according to plan.[34]

Qn: Can you tell me who you are?
Teacher: I will tell you at a later time. I do not wish to compromise my position.

Qn: Thank you for visiting us this evening.
Teacher: It has been my pleasure. I have not done this for a while, for a long, long while. Think about what I have told you, for when your mind gets around these facts it will grow in understanding. Until you have a grasp of it, can I ask that you keep your knowledge to yourselves? As your understanding grows, your ability to communicate it as it should be communicated will grow; then you may put out certain things.

The Source – Second conversation

Qn: Is there one Ultimate Source?

---

34   This is also addressed in the Section titled 'Life Paths in the Physical'.

Teacher: This I have confirmed already[35]. There is only one Ultimate Source.

Qn: What is the Ultimate Source? Can you describe it in simple words?
Teacher: Energy.

Qn: Energy?
Teacher: Energy and vibration. More energy.

Qn: Is it a mix of colours or anything else, or is it a mix of vibrations?
Teacher: Energy in its purist form. The Individual Sources that look after individual areas of the Universe, that have previously referred to as son and daughter Sources for want of an understandable description, vibrate at different frequencies and are different types of energy. But the Ultimate Source of all is pure energy, it vibrates above the rest.

Qn: Is it an accumulation of history or has the energy just created...
Teacher: The energy was here from the start; it is not yet within your comprehension. I could describe it, but you do not yet have the understanding this time. I hope you can live with this for a while.

Qn: Where is the Ultimate Source?
Teacher: A good question, it is everywhere.

Qn: Is that because we are made up from energy belonging to the Ultimate Source?
Teacher: All our energy can be absorbed within the Ultimate Source, but you are not of the same Level as the Ultimate Source or vibrating at his level.

---

35 This had previously been addressed in the first conversation the Circle had with Teacher and demonstrated consistency in the answers being given.

Qn: How old is the Ultimate Source?
Teacher: As old as time itself.

Qn: Is the Ultimate Source visible and to whom is it visible?
Teacher: The Ultimate Source is only visible to those who can see, for its light would be too bright for us on this plane to see.

Qn: When I pass into spirit, will I be able to see or feel the Ultimate Source?
Teacher: You will be able to feel the Ultimate Source. You will not be able to see it. As you progress and become closer to the Ultimate Source then you might stand a chance of seeing it.

Qn: At Level 2 can you see the Ultimate Source or are you part of it?
Teacher: You are becoming part of the Source, for at that Level you tend to lose your identity. You then become more of……. a Conglomerate, is that the word? A 'joining' is the better word.

Qn: Has the Ultimate Source created life, of both physical and spiritual matter?
Teacher: Energy created life. The spreading out of things, for at first there was pure energy and from that came…. Can you comprehend that?

Qn: Where does the understanding of a blackhole fit in?
Teacher: It sucks the energy. It sucks everything within it.

Qn: And was that created from the pure energy that you say we have got?
Teacher: It is the natural generation of things. For when things are created things must be removed.

Qn: Balanced?
Teacher: All is in balance.

Qn: So, should we be wary of blackhole energy?
Teacher: It does not affect you. It is not within your Solar System.

Qn: Is that part of the balance that you refer to?
Teacher: It balances the structure of the Universe. There are energies that are not as bright as others that tend to suck in more than they should have, but we work tirelessly to keep the perfect balance.

Qn: Does the Ultimate Source wish to be worshipped or recognised and loved for its creation?
Teacher: To be loved, to be recognised, and in some way appreciated. And now that some religions wish to worship the Source that is their own path too, as it satisfies their emotional needs, for their faith is all that is needed as recognition that there is a Source.

Qn: Is the Ultimate Source all seeing and hearing, or does it rely on teams to monitor what happens on the physical and spiritual planes?
Teacher: It is everywhere but also having emissaries to keep an eye on things. For example, there are monitors that help to keep an eye out and assist where possible and report back to the Source to allow there to be contact.

Qn: Would that be at Angel Level in the spirit world?
Teacher: It is at different Levels this occurs, and reporting goes up through the Levels. Also, if a Source wishes to make contact in some way, there are the emissaries. To do that, it will appoint somebody to make contact to pass a message to a particular person.

Qn: Does the Ultimate Source have the ability to destroy its creations?
Teacher: Why would it wish to destroy its creations? Everything

has its time and when that time has come for this Earth to finish, the Ultimate Source will absorb every life-force[36], none will be left behind, and will find a new home and begin again. You need never fear that it will all end.

Qn: Should the Ultimate Source have concerns about mankind's progress?
Teacher: Mankind has its path before it. They hope that they will reach that point, but they will not.

Qn: So, does the Ultimate Source cross inter-dimensions?
Teacher: The Ultimate Source can cross all dimensions.

Qn: Does the Ultimate Source support all dimensions, like other planets?
Teacher: There are other Individual Sources[37].

Qn: Is there a separate Individual Source for each planet or each Universe or Galaxy?
Teacher: For each System, each dimension is different. The energy is slightly different. To explain to you in simple terms – if the energy within our Individual Source area is gold, the energy around another Individual Source area could be blue or green. That is very simplistic, and I hope you can understand. It would not be easy to cross between the two because the energies are so different. But you may do that through the Ultimate Source, who has the ability…

---

36 The Teacher is referring to the spiritual energy of the life force.

37 The Teacher is referring to the other Individual Sources (elsewhere referred to as son or daughter Sources) that have been mentioned and which have responsibility for their own areas, maybe Galaxies or larger rather than Solar Systems.

Qn: The Ultimate Source can be some form of gateway?
Teacher: The Ultimate Source may, if your desire is to explore new dimensions, then your energy can be swapped with another Individual Source to stay in balance.

Qn: Does that mean a spirit energy cannot leave unless another energy comes here?
Teacher: All must be balanced. Individual Sources have links with each other, like you have links between you, they come from the same creation.

Qn: How do the other Individual Sources exist?
Teacher: In their own areas, like ours exist within this area. You must remember that you cannot see all that is out there, even with the strongest telescope you may not see all that is out there.

Qn: I think the term for transporting is 'apports'? How does that travel through the Ultimate Source and how does that occur through energy?
Teacher: You can alter the vibration of things. Once the vibration of something is altered, it will pass through many things. So, you take the thing and alter its vibration till it passes through a solid structure and then return the vibration to its correct level and the 'apport' comes out of the energy.

Qn: When this thing travels through a solid structure, is it just the thing that is affected or both?
Teacher: The energy of the thing can pass through in its own right.

Qn: The solid structure stays solid?
Teacher: The solid structure is vibrating.

Qn: Does the energy pass through the spaces in the atoms?
Teacher: Through the atoms, otherwise we would need to make big holes in everything. It is very similar to turning your hand to jelly, they alter the vibrations and the structure alters. Alter it enough and you can pass it through things, like solids, liquid and gases.

My friends, I have been here a while now, I think I must bid you farewell. I have enjoyed being here, thank you for inviting me. I must ask until your understanding becomes fuller not to pass on information, and I know your Guides will keep this to themselves until a better understanding is reached in the fullness of time. You may pass on some information only when you can pass information that you can fully answer questions on.

After the Teacher's second visit, members of the Circle started raising questions relating to the structure of the spirit world. Of course, its structure and development may be an evolution of a separate creation within the Universe that we cannot see and know nothing about. However, discussing its structure and evolution did become an interesting topic for conversation. It is at this point I change the visiting spirit's description from Teacher to Conglomerate based on the earlier descriptive information that had been given.

The Source – Third conversation

Conglomerate: My friends, how can I help you this evening?

Qn: You have said that the Ultimate Source started from the beginning of time. Are you able to give some idea how the Ultimate Source was created?
Conglomerate: I do not think you could comprehend this at this point. For it is hard even for us to understand.

Qn: That is like what you had said before. But you also said it is pure energy and vibration. Did it need a companion or mate, or any kind of mixture to expand?
Conglomerate: Do you mean to create?

Qn: Yes.
Conglomerate: It needed to focus upon its creation because the energy was already there before the creation.

Qn: Was the energy in some form of vacuum?
Conglomerate: The energy crosses dimensions. Your dimension was not here at that time, but others were. Yours was not the first. This is where it may become difficult for you to understand.

Qn: Can you describe it in a simple way? Was it some small energy buzzing around?
Conglomerate: No, it was a blast of inter-dimensional energy that created this dimension. It is as if it came through a Veil, I know this is hard to comprehend, can you follow? If not, I must try to simplify it even more. Can you follow what I have said?

Qn: It is the moment of suddenness that I am having a little difficulty understanding.
Conglomerate: Can you imagine a Veil, a barrier, and an explosion of energy through that barrier creating a focus of energy within your part of the Universe and sparking the creation of what you know now. But it did not come originally from this dimension. Can you follow that?

Qn: When the Energy came through the Veil did it pass through without damaging the Veil? Did it come through the molecular structure?

Conglomerate: It was dimension into dimension. No tears, no damage, but focused and intended.[38]

Qn: That's what scientists call the big bang, but they have no concept of how it happened yet. Is this the sort of thing that would have happened for the creation of our Individual Source?
Conglomerate: They came with it. They came to establish.

Qn: So, the Ultimate Source did not create us, it was part of a knock-on effect.
Conglomerate: No, it created. It supplied the conditions that were needed to create what we have, for is it not magnificent what has been created?

Qn: Absolutely. Were the different spirit Levels and life created by our Individual Source?
Conglomerate: Yes. They are responsible for the energy of creation.

Qn: So, Individual Sources are specifically responsible for their environment and what goes on in their environment?
Conglomerate: They are responsible for the existence within their environment, and all develop as they decide. It is their responsibility.

Qn: The fact that an Individual Source has a world that exists within it, does a similar world exist within the Ultimate Source?
Conglomerate: No.

---

38 The Veil is not a visible object. It is a word that is being used to describe what happens as the vibrations of individual spirits, and those who transition back to spirits, change. Passing through the Veil is also used in conversations that were held with other spirits in the Section titled 'Transitioning between Worlds'.

Qn: The Ultimate Source exists on its own and has no world that exists within it?
Conglomerate: It has entire worlds within it.

Qn: Does that mean it has entire Solar Systems, Galaxies, within it?
Conglomerate: The Ultimate Source is responsible for all around it.

Qn: So that's all the other Galaxies or Solar Systems as well?
Conglomerate: Yes.

Qn: Within these worlds, do you have the spirit world, the physical plane and the Individual Source itself?
Conglomerate: The Source is part of the structure.

Qn: Where does the Ultimate Source store its knowledge? Where do the Individual Sources store their knowledge?
Conglomerate: Within their collective being.

Qn: What is a collective being?
Conglomerate: I will try to make it easier for you to understand. You have a higher consciousness.[39] This higher consciousness is part of your spiritual energy and being that can store endless information. When they are absorbed within a Source, all that information is stored within that Source. I am trying to think of a way that I can explain it simply. Just let me concentrate and find a way you will understand.

A molecule of water remembers it is a molecule of water even when it is thrown into a puddle. Within the puddle that molecule of water is still an individual molecule but collectively it becomes a puddle. If you take that puddle and throw it into a lake it is still a

---

[39] Higher consciousness is also addressed in more detail in the Section titled 'Higher Consciousness (and Memory)'.

molecule of water, and the puddle is still a puddle, and now it exists within a lake. It has not changed its nature but has been absorbed by the lake; it still has its memory of being a molecule of water. It has not lost its identity but has been absorbed into the greater identity. It has become one as a lake, but it has its memory of being a molecule of water absorbed by the lake.

Qn: You have said the path of some individuals may be to attain being absorbed into the Ultimate Source. Would they be absorbed by their Individual Source first?
Conglomerate: Yes, that is correct.

Qn: Can an Individual Source be absorbed by the Ultimate Source?
Conglomerate: Yes, that is correct.

Qn: There is a hierarchy?
Conglomerate: Yes, there is. For without a hierarchy chaos would exist.

Qn: You have said previously that sometimes the Ultimate Source may visit people and may leave a mark. What type of mark and what is left behind? Is it scarring?
Conglomerate: No, but the energy that is the Ultimate Source is very strong, and it will only come through somebody who can cope with the energy that it carries. You may be left with a severe hangover that could last days.

Qn: Would it be harmful?
Conglomerate: No, just would be left energy. But if this were the case, he would arrange a Medium, he would arrange to communicate across a third party, so his energy is not in direct contact with the person he is communicating with. You would feel it. He is very strong.

Qn: Does it leave a residual energy change for that individual until they go back to the spirit world? Is there some residual energy left or impact from that visit? Is that the scarring you talk about?

Conglomerate: Energy is left. It is not a physical scar as it is the energy that is left. Vibration of the individual remains the same. To a Medium, you would see the difference and would be able to see that differential you would be feeling, that is all. He would come like a blanket and just swamp your mind and in those seconds read everything, situation, history, that which is all and everything, and when he reads your mind, you may know he has visited by the hangover that you would be left with; it is not going to harm you but might be very uncomfortable for a few days after. He would only do that to those that can take it, although he could adjust if he wished to. He would get somebody else in if it would mean he would have to make a big adjustment. So usually, he would use a third party.

Qn: Thank you.

Conglomerate: I think my time is coming to an end now. It was a pleasure.

The Source – Fourth conversation

Visitor[40]: I am almost here; they are adjusting us to a new dimension. Different dimensions require different energy to cover everywhere. The new room is more acceptable for development as it provides more space than the smaller room. It provides a picture like on your television on a small screen, and now we are on a big picture screen. The dimension, size, and the broadcast need to be adjusted for this bigger room[41]. That's better, I think, I am settled.

---

40 Sometimes the visits from the Conglomerate were preceded by a spirit that seemed to be checking the surroundings are all they should be.

41 This was an unexpected statement, and one that I cannot explain. ☛

Qn: Do we have the Teacher or Conglomerate visiting?
Visitor: You have a single Entity here; I have come to check the surroundings before bringing the others with me. Next time we will come as a whole, but for now you have a single Entity. Can I help you?

Qn: We are hoping to continue with the questions from the Conglomerate's last visit.
Single Entity: I will do my best, for there is more knowledge within the group than within a single Entity. Please ask.

Qn: We have been told that the Ultimate Source is singular and that worlds only exist within Individual Sources. This evening, can we focus on the Source for our part of the Universe[42].
Single Entity: The Individual Source?

Qn: Yes, how many Levels are there?
Single Entity: Twelve.

Qn: What purpose do these Levels serve and why were they created?
Single Entity: This is an easy question; the Levels allow for progression of spirit and for compactivity.

Qn: What does that mean?
Single Entity: Because they vibrate differently on each of the different Levels, they will all fit within the same space, I should say.[43]

    Only days before, I had not given any warning of my intent to transfer the location of the library to a larger spare room in which we could accommodate more visitors in comfortable surroundings. It had not entered my head that I would be changing the dimensions for spirits to work in.

42   The Solar System or Galaxy where Earth is located.

43   The Single Entity is referring to the multi-dimensional structure of the

Qn: Were those Levels created purposely as a structure, or did they just evolve?
Single Entity: The evolved structure for these Levels was already there. But in the beginning, there were not so many Levels that had been filled so with time and development the Levels grew to fulfil the destined number.

Qn: Does this mean that if it becomes overcrowded any time in the future that you will create more Levels?
Single Entity: No, because the final Level is absorption into the one Ultimate Source, so the Levels will never become overcrowded. Also, the amount of space that an individual takes up is miniscule within the entirety of the system.

Qn: Do the Levels exist together without collision?
Single Entity: Yes. Because they are all of a different vibration level, they can co-exist but do not intermingle.

Qn: Can each Level see the other?
Single Entity: No, though some individuals of the higher vibration level can see down through all the Levels.

Qn: Is this because they are allowed to?
Single Entity: They have the ability; some can see the layers below. As individual spirits develop, most will live within their Level happily and content until they discover there is something beyond this; until they decide they wish to develop and take on a fuller part within the system. For example, working as a Guide to another individual to watch over and protect that individual's development and to assist only where necessary, unless it is a Medium.

---

spirit world that can exist within itself.

Qn: Do the structures differ between different Individual Sources, and how?
Single Entity: The structures differ. You cannot just go from one Individual Source to another as the vibration and wavelengths of each are different. The energy is also different, just slightly. Because of the vibration levels it is like, as I believe we have said before, if your colour is yellow, then their colour could be red. The difference is like, mountains of difference.

Qn: I am curious to know whether other Individual Sources also have twelve Levels? I do understand the vibration differences.
Single Entity: I do not know the answer to that because I have not been privileged to visit other Individual Sources. Some do visit us from other Sources[44]; I will inquire for you.

Qn: Have our spirit and physical worlds evolved over time?
Single Entity: All evolves over time, nothing stays still.

Qn: Is anyone directing progress within the environment of our Individual Source?
Single Entity: There are those that oversee the development of the Earth plane.

Qn: Who are they?
Single Entity: They are various and many.

Qn: Have they existed for a long time? Have they visited the physical plane?
Single Entity: They have visited. Some have existed from time beginning to watch and work with the Source. They are the Source's right hand, so to speak. I believe we have explained it before.

---

44   This is briefly mentioned in the Section titled 'Life in the Universe'.

Qn: Are there many?
Single Entity: There are many that have joined the ranks of the few over time. For in the beginning there was not the need for so many because development was very slow.

Qn: Is this part of evolution of both the spiritual and physical worlds in balance together?
Single Entity: Yes. All must progress, for all things evolve within the spirit world as well as the physical world and all those that return from the Earth into the spiritual world bring more advancement. Overall, spirits will have advanced their individual self and so they will bring with them their own advancement. All must evolve to survive within the planet. Within the spiritual world one must evolve, not to survive[45], but to keep up with the changes to physical world.

Qn: When you progress through the Levels in the spirit world how does the spirit change?
Single Entity: It vibrates at a different level.

Qn: How does that happen? Who chooses it to vibrate at that greater level to progress?
Single Entity: You do not get to choose it, if you progress your vibration changes. That is how you change Levels, or progress within the Level. Your vibration slowly advances within a Level until you reach the next Level, provided you continue to develop and have not chosen to stay within that area.

Qn: Is it noticeable?
Single Entity: You would notice it, but it would be a natural

---

45   Because the lifetime of the spiritual energy is infinite.

progression. If you are trying to progress, you would be happy to feel an increase in vibration.

Qn: The Earth is advancing its knowledge. Is the same happening for the spirit world?
Single Entity: Of course. Those that are Guides are learning all the time, and they are practicing new techniques. For example, something you are familiar with, a Guide that guides a Medium can come through and learn new techniques to show themselves that they did not know in the Victorian era, they have progressed.

Qn: Is the spirit world evolving with communication?
Single Entity: Yes, and you must remember those that leave the physical world take with them that which they have learned on Earth, enabling and setting up communes of like-minded people and so it develops and the knowledge spreads.

Qn: Is everything pure within the spirit world?
Single Entity: Nowhere but the highest Levels is there purity. I think you have already experienced this.

Qn: Is there negativity in the lowest Level areas in the spirit world?
Single Entity: Always balanced, but it is protected within these areas.

Qn: Has our Individual Source ever experienced the physical world?
Single Entity: In its creation it feels and seems different. It has not, other than in spirit, walked upon this Earth.

The Source – Fifth conversation

Qn: Do we have the Teacher with us now?
Conglomerate: I am settled, and my energy has been adjusted.

Qn: It has been said there is a barrier between the physical and spiritual worlds and the individual Source because of the layers. Are these layers impenetrable, will they ever be breached?
Conglomerate: The barrier between the physical world and the spiritual world will not be breached by the physical body. The physical body cannot go into the spiritual world. But the spirit world can come into the physical body.

Qn: Were the different Levels or layers created because there are so many spirits, and you needed to create space and dimensions?
Conglomerate: Levels and layers have been created for development not because there were too many spirits. It was created to allow the spirits to grow, to grow nearer to the Creator, to take their own place in the scheme of things and once they become aware that there is more…. do you not wish to look over the garden fence? Do you not wish to know what is going on just out of sight? For if you did not wish to know, why do you travel, why do you pick up a book to read, and why do you watch things grow?

Qn: Regarding development to grow nearer to the Source, who chooses a spirit's development and how can they grow?
Conglomerate: It is when spirits become aware that there is more and when they see further, they choose to progress on. Some wish to help others, some wish to help humanity, some wish to teach. Just like within your planet you have desires to do things, so spirits have desires to do things and if you start, for example as a student teacher, you will not wish to stay on as a student teacher all your life would you? You would aspire to the next Level and when that is achieved you remain there for a length of time learning more, acquiring new skills, helping to do various things within your chosen desire and then eventually you become promoted to the next position and so you aspire to become head teacher.

Qn: Is each Level fixed? I mean – to achieve Level 4, do you help people; to achieve Level 5, do you help mankind. What must you do?
Conglomerate: There is a certain amount of flexibility, but there are also a certain number of criteria and things that must be met. Things that are set and weighed.

Qn: Is that mostly knowledge or the things we do?
Conglomerate: It is based on knowledge gained because you are learning by experience, and by helping others you gain knowledge and experience. So, it would come down ultimately to knowledge. Everything you do gives you knowledge, but also what you do with your knowledge does help your cause. If you just sat there and did nothing you would stay sitting there doing nothing for eternity and that would be a terrible shame, and a terrible waste of time allotted.

Qn: The terminology of going through the Veil has come up several times. Is the Veil the description of what separates each of the Levels.
Conglomerate: It is a very good description.

Qn: I understand that each of the Levels are at different vibrations. Does it get brighter as you move up through these Levels?
Conglomerate: The lowest Level is here on Earth, and it could not be light because if it was you would never have darkness when you close your eyes.

Qn: Do Spirits get brighter as they progress through the Levels, and when they come together in communities create light for themselves?
Conglomerate: They are all light and energy. But, as on this Earth, there are different levels of aspiration. Some aspire higher than others, some aspire higher and faster than others, but all become close, and it depends on their own level of acceleration.

Qn: When we pass from the physical plane, will our vibration be the same if we have not achieved the path or goal to an increased Level?
Conglomerate: It is not core dependent on one goal. Progress depends on where you were on the Level when you came back down to Earth. If you had only just started up on that Level, it may not take you all the way to the next Level but will progress you higher through the Level you were at, so that you have gone from the base vibrations to a higher difference. Each area is like a bandwidth. Do you understand the term bandwidth?

Qn: Yes.
Conglomerate: Each area has a width of band. When you first enter you vibrate at that band and as you progress your vibration level increases until you obtain the vibration level that enables you to cross through the Veil into the base level of the next band. You cannot just go. Your vibration level needs to be raised and this you do by progressing through the Level you are already at.

Qn: Is the Veil a line that separates things or is the Veil just a different terminology for the different Levels?
Conglomerate: It is a terminology to describe the barriers between the Levels in the spirit world.

Qn: A slight change of subject, but still about the Individual Source. Is your Conglomerate part of a Council that may make decisions about the Earth?
Conglomerate: Let us put it this way, we are not one of the Prophets. But we do our best to supply knowledge and we may be called upon very, very occasionally. When we have been called, how wonderful, and it is just for a little bit of information that we can supply. But we do not make the decisions, it is not our position. It is for those on the highest Levels to make the decision about the Earth. There are those nearer to the Earth that make decisions about various

mundane things, like who the Guides are going to be, which life are you going to go into, what is it that you wish to attain, what is it you wish to experience, are you happy going there, do you think you can cope with that life, could it bring you what you want to know, could it bring you what you want to learn. These are more everyday mundane, but the higher decisions are made a lot higher. You would expect that. It is a great privilege to be called before the Council to be involved, even in just a smidgen of a way it is a great privilege. Of course, the main Teacher does the talking then, it is his rank, and he has seniority. But we all attend together as one group, and if he does not know, he is not so proud that he does not turn to one of us and says this is your field can you lend assistance. Of course, we step up to say I can help, I can offer this advice; I can offer this information.

Qn: Is this for planned Events?
Conglomerate: This is for Knowledge. Because of our studies, our love of knowledge, experience, and our libraries of books, we have more of an encompassing knowledge, and so we are called upon to supply usually just something to do with small things that they have not yet got quite a grasp of, or they may want to know how something would affect what was already known.

There is quite a lot of information to absorb for those who are exploring spirit knowledge for the first time, and even some with greater experience and knowledge of spirit may have found the conversations challenging to understand. So below, I have tried to give headline and bullet point summaries of the key points of the conversations. You can read more about how spirits cross through the Veils when moving between the various Levels, exist in the various Levels, transition from physical back to spirit, etc. in the various Sections that follow.

Concept of the Ultimate Source:

The Ultimate Source is described as a singular creation entity that controls multiple Individual Sources, each with responsibility for their own areas within the Universe, all operating with the same energy and love. The Individual Sources each sustain their own areas, and these may be construed as galaxies or multiple galaxies.

Energy-Based Existence:

The Ultimate Source and everything else in the Universe are explained as being energy-based, with even the most solid objects being made up of energy. The energy vibrates and the rates of vibration define the dimension or spirit Level.

Spiritual Progression:

Spirits, if they so wish, can be absorbed into the Ultimate Source. By doing so, they lose their singular identity and become part of the greater energy. This may be the ultimate objective for some spirits.

Communication with the Ultimate Source:

The Ultimate Source may communicate with any level of existence and may also be made aware of much through its emissaries or Individual Sources.

Creation and Balance:

The Ultimate Source is considered to be created of energy, which in turn created life and maintains balance within the Universe, including phenomena like black holes as part of a regeneration process.

Role of Individual Sources:

Individual Sources are responsible for their own environments within the Universe and the development within them, while the Ultimate Source oversees everything.

Levels of Spiritual Existence:

There are twelve Levels of spiritual existence within our Individual Source area, each allowing for the progression of spirits to move upwards towards the Ultimate Source, if that is their desire, with every step increase in their own vibration and purpose. Each Level also has sub-divisions or vibration ranges to enable progression within the Level.

Evolution of the Spirit World:

The spirit world continues to evolve, with spirits advancing through the Levels based on their knowledge and experiences attained within physical and spiritual worlds, and also in a similar way in which the physical world has progressed over time.

Hierarchy in the Spirit World:

There is a hierarchy in the spirit world, with councils and emissaries making decisions, guiding progress, ensuring order and balance, and on-going development within the area.

The Realms

The Chief emphasised the importance of incorporating a section about the three realms. Given that I was working under guidance from the Chief, I did not feel that I could decline his request despite not being familiar with the concept of spirit realms. Thus, I considered it would be prudent to allow the Chief to speak first on the subject, after which the Circle could ask questions and then I could verify the information later. The English Oxford Dictionary defines a realm as a kingdom (an archaic term), or a field or domain of activity of interest. However, there are various alternative interpretations for the description of a realm, depending on the context or group to which it is applied.

So, what are the realms according to those in the spirit world? From the ensuing discussion, it is evident that spirits have their own interpretation of these realms, including their composition, location, and application to life.

Chief: There are three realms where life is supported, and you must ask about them.

Qn: Where are these three realms?
Chief: They are all within your reach.

Qn: What are they?
Chief: There is much talk about naming these. They are often

referred to by Mediums as the realms of Us[46], the Universe, as well as the angelic realm.

Qn: Are you referring now to the three spiritual Realms?
Chief: No. Not all, just the human perception of this area. There may be three realms that are referred to, but within this are also many divisions. So, the concept of the three realms is very simplistic and gives the unenlightened mind some grasp of it, but the reality is that each area is far more complex and has significant inner divisions. These divisions are worth exploring in the interest of the reader[47].

The first realm refers to the 'Earth and the physical' that is divided into many living and perceived non-living things[48] – the vibration varies across all of the Earth in items and structure. This also refers to those in this part of the Universe that is your small existence.

Next you have the 'wider Universe' where there are different stages of development with others looking after those areas. Hence the Universe has a Job Title or star people[49], although of course, they are not all people. The divisions are many and varied.

Then we get to the 'spirit realm', often referred to as the angelic realm. In simplistic terms, you already know of the many divisions[50]

---

46 The realm of 'Us' is being applied to the area that linked to the physical Earth within the Universe.

47 The word of the Chief, not mine, for inclusion in this book.

48 The reference to perceived non-living things is that which we perceive to have no life, perhaps rocks, water, etc. but which spirit tell us still has its own vibrating energy.

49 Star People – another reference (8 years after being mentioned by the Conglomerate) to the existence of other energies and life within the wider Universe. This is something that I hope to explore at later time.

50 This is referring to the different Levels and vibrations that exist within the spirit realm, and within each Level there are also differing 'bandwidths' of energy. This was also previously addressed in conversations with the Conglomerate and with other spirit visitors in later Sections.

within this and of the layers within these divisions.

Qn: If you take the Universe structure as being Galaxy, Solar System, Planet. Is that applied Universe wide?
Chief: Yes, in the second part of the trio of realms and included in all.

Qn: We have previously been told that there is the Ultimate Source, and the son and daughter (Individual) Sources which I believe refer to Galaxies or Solar Systems.
Chief: Wider.

Qn: Within each of those, are there combinations of physical life. (Yes). And life that is spiritual or energy based. (Yes). Is there life that has developed as a physical spiritual life, in other words a physical life existence where they are much closer to their energy.
Chief: Yes. The same could happen with this physical world, but there is too much learning needed. As you, forgive me ..., we have learnt that we are still primitive despite the years of advancement.

Qn: Can you clarify the spiritual Levels of the third Realm, please. Is Level 1 or 12 the Ultimate Source?
Chief: Does not matter what Level you call it, Level 1 or 12, it is still the Source. Level 2 or 11 is Masters.

Qn: What is Level 3 or 10?
Chief: Here it is Level 1 for the Source. That is the most widely understood reference.

Qn: What does the lowest Level look like in spirit?
Chief: Black and Earth like.

Qn: What is the next Level down from the Masters?
Chief: Level 3, the angels.

Qn: Beneath that?
Chief: Many different levels of vibration.

Qn: If you were describing angels from the angelic Level, what are they?
Chief: They are energies that have developed to a level where they can help and influence events.

∾

The discussion diverged slightly as the Circle sought a deeper comprehension of the various Levels within the spirit realm and a more precise description of these numerous perceived divisions. I had not grasped the Chief's reference to the Universe having a 'Job Title' and waited until the next session to request further clarification, the answers to which were subsequently provided by the Conglomerate.

Qn: What is meant by "the Universe has a Job Title".
Conglomerate: The Universe is so large that it can only be referred to as a unifying Title, and to break that down would mean too many divisions that you could fill a book by just stating those individual divisions that it has. So, for ease of reference, it is often given an encompassing Job Lot as a title. I hope that helps. You have come a long way in your thirst for knowledge.

Qn: Is there information you can give on this subject that might help further?
Conglomerate: Let me help you understand the Universe a little better. You now understand that everything is energy and is vibrating

no matter how slow. But if you consider ants, their individual colonies number trillions across this planet. They are varied and they exist near to one another or across vast distances, e.g. water. There is a similarity to the size and distance across the Universe, and this may help you expand your mind by relating to the size and distance and numbers across the Universe. If I give you this metaphor, can you now grasp what I am saying.

Qn: Yes. Thank you.
Conglomerate: You are welcome. Our lives have intertwined now for years, and I feel that I know you well my friend. I will come more often to give you inspiration to fill in gaps for your book.

The Light

What is the Light? Numerous accounts from spirit visitors consistently claimed the Light as their home in the spirit realm, it is the destination for all individual spirits upon leaving their physical bodies at the time of death.

Understanding the events that will occur at the time of an individual's physical death and what happens thereafter can provide significant comfort to grieving family and loved ones. Though I doubt there is one fit for all, it is important to consider what can truly be expected when the time comes for an individual to leave their physical body. Will they be able to recognise the Light? Is the Light going to be easily distinguishable from sunlight or moonlight, which they have been accustomed to in the physical realm? Will they still be able to recognise their surroundings? What measures can be taken to ensure that their newly liberated spirit remains free and does not become confined to the physical realm? Alternatively, is the newly liberated spirit automatically directed or drawn into a bright light that leads or deposits the individual in the next realm? These are some of the questions I wanted to find answers to.

I wanted to understand the significance that spirits attribute to each newly liberated spirit returning to the Light. To achieve this, I asked visiting spirits to share some of their experiences and recollections relating to before and after they entered the Light and whether they continue to reside there. Shortly before collecting this information, there was an unexpected visit by

Joel from the Conglomerate, who requested that I include this precautionary message regarding the conversations we would be having with spirits on this and other subjects. His message emphasises the importance of acknowledging that some answers given are based on the varied experiences of individual spirits who exist within different Levels or bandwidths of the spirit world.

Joel: My name is Joel from Conglomerate. I am here to give guidance to this Circle. I am sure that you all feel that any guidance is welcome but that means you need to be selective with what you take forward. You must remember, it is always from that person's own perspective, and they are telling you as they see it. It is like for someone who never leaves their town their perspective will be narrow compared to that of someone who has travelled and lived elsewhere in the UK as well. Then there is the person who has travelled around Europe as well, and their knowledge and perspective will be even greater. Then there is the person who has travelled and lived around the world as well as all the other things and their perspectives are greatly enhanced over everyone else's.

Qn: When you refer to perspective, how far is that perspective around that individual?
Joel: It depends on their exposure and development.

Qn: Can you give me an example, between those spirits residing on Level 3 and those on Level 8?
Joel: The difference is huge. Level 3 vibrations are for those with the least understanding. If you are at Level 8 you are nearer to the Source of knowledge and understanding, therefore you will have greater knowledge and be nearer to the Source in vibration.

The intervention was timely and demonstrated that spirits were also observing progress and providing more assistance than I had previously been prepared to recognise. I guess this assistance also helps to ensure the accuracy of the information being presented in this book, and it is something that I fully appreciate. Furthermore, at the time of Joel's visit, no one within the Circle was aware of my intention to write about the Light and include some conversations with spirits from the various Levels.

Chief: You and our visitors are interested in the Light. This is where you cross the area and enter through the Veil by way of a light energy bridge[51]. This energy is the Creators love, and we all feel it and add to it with our radiating love. We can enter into the world beyond through this medium, it allows us to mix and meet and live with our loved ones.

If, and when you pass to the Light, we try to make your arrival into the Light as a least traumatic experience. It should be somewhere you will be comfortable with and that you feel safe and appreciated to join us in the Realms of your forefathers and those that came before you, where you will feel their welcome and the love.

Qn: Can you tell me more about the Light.
Chief: The Light is the energy of the Creator; it gives us the power to

---

51   By referring to a bridge between physical and spiritual worlds the Chief is metaphorically describing the connection between two worlds or dimensions that are separated by a Veil. Passing through the Veil does not mean that you have passed into the Light, just that you will have left your physical body and entered a world of spirit energy. Leaving the physical body frees your energy to increase its vibration, and as you disappear from the physical world so a new world in spirit will appear. Hence the descriptive term – crossing through a Veil.

exist. All the things you see in this physical world are held together by a fine mechanism, upset that and you have breakdown. What you see around you is governed by your physical eyes that have limited sight values. They can only show you what they are capable of seeing, but your spirit eyes, so to speak, see on a different level, they are capable of different dimensions of sight that your physical eyes cannot comprehend. Your spirit eyes are able to see entire worlds beyond your physical eyes, for their energy and vibration levels are different.

Qn: Is time infinite in the Light?
Chief: There is a symbol that means all of time and distance. You may think that analogy is quite strange, but you see, time is infinite so the measure of it in the Light is not possible. On Earth, you only measure the passing of the sun and moon, and this also applies to your seasons that you measure by the nature world around you. You must understand there are no fixed times in the Universe, only on this speck of a planet. You create your own treadmill, and you create your own timescale which helps your existence but only applies to this speck of dust in the Universe. If you disregard this time constraint you will get more of an understanding of what your home life is like when you return.

Qn: When a person first passes through the Veil, do they pass over at the same vibration level? (Yes). Are they still at the same vibration level when at the doorway to the Light.
Chief: No. You will have left your tie to the physical by then and are free to grow into yourself.

Qn: When you enter the Light, is that the point at which a person's vibration changes as they move through the Veil? (Yes). As you spend time in the Light, do you find your original or natural level of vibration.

Chief: Your level that you are comfortable with, that you have achieved.

Qn: Is the Light governed by the number of spirits existing in the Light? (No). Is the Light very bright? (Yes). What or who governs the strength of the Light?
Chief: The Creator.

Qn: If there are more spirits within the Light, does this cause the brightness to fluctuate? (No). Are spirits in eternal darkness if they don't go into the Light?
Chief: No, they remain in the physical world, the first Level. It is difficult because they become stuck in your world.

Qn: If a spirit doesn't go to the Light will they still experience night and day? (No). Will they see everything set in darkness? (No). Will this vary from spirit to spirit? (Yes). Can you describe being in the Light?
Chief: I will talk about this as a universal energy of love. This has often been referred to by erudite and scholars with little understanding of the power of love. It brings connections across the Universe and across its people and population. There is little understanding of what it is like to stand in a field of energy driven by love from the Creator downwards. We are capable of sensing only a small proportion of this love. We find it connects us to individuals. I am not talking about biological lust for that is for the survival of the races, I am talking about the pure joy and love that you can happily exist in forever and that can be felt amongst each and every one present in those realms. There is an undeniable need within all those that subconsciously miss the love that they have known, and it calls them to search as such for it on Earth.

Qn: Are spirits living their lives the same in the Light?
Chief: We are multifaith, and non-attached. We have broadened your horizons beyond the accepted norms.

Qn: You refer to spirits being of multifaith and non-attached, can you explain please?
Chief: It means we are all recognising the true Prophets for their importance in the development of our thoughts and existence, and we recognise the Creator as above all others in this world's existence, and it means that we live in harmony once we progress beyond the third Level[52]. I think that once all the barriers of release come down, the peace and reconciliation bring harmony, and you feel that there are no longer the barriers that man puts up on the Earth plane.

Qn: We are told there are 12 Levels. (Yes). Are the first 9 Levels where spirits spend their everyday spiritual lives, and the three highest Levels are not for everyday living. (No).

Qn: Are you saying that the first three Levels from the Earth plane upwards means that people still must adjust to reach the harmonious Levels in spirit?
Chief: Yes. Only those lives past the third Level are in harmony.

Qn: Does this mean that in the first three Levels individuals are still sorting out their faith or beliefs. (Yes). And the top three Levels are not ordinary life, because that is where the prophets, angels and Creator exist. (Yes).

---

52   I found this statement quite interesting and enlightening. Taken into context with other answers, within the 12 Levels there seems to be 6 Levels of middling progression bordered by 3 Levels at either side consisting of lower and higher levels of varied spiritual vibrations.

Qn: I was wondering whether there is the kind of relationship in the Light that we have on the physical Earth.

Conglomerate: Yes. You carry love with you when you go into the Light. That love does not die, it stays so that relationships that you may have in the physical world, do in the spirit world, stay with you. You are privileged to be able to do that. You are privileged to achieve all that you do achieve, because love is not allowed to be shown so freely in the physical world. You are constrained within your society in terms of how you can behave. But the Light is based on love, so your love can be shown and radiated to those that are with you, and relationships are much stronger there. You can make relationships on many visits to this Earth and those relationships will still stay strong, and you will also have the relationships that you form within the spirit world. Within your community, you form bonds that are strong, and those bonds are a privilege to have. On the Earth, here you are restrained to how you live your life, how you mix with people. You may see a person that you feel you would get along with, but you would not go over to them and say I would love to get to know you better. You have not been introduced the proper way, not part of your group or society and you do not say this unless you were a gentleman chatting up someone. In the spirit world, if you wish to get to know a person, you will go up to them and say I would like to know you better on a friendship basis and they would be delighted to respond. I have been privileged to have had many friendships and relationships throughout my existence, and I am privileged to be able to enjoy those relationships to this day. You see, it is a blessing to be in a society where love is the most important thing. You do not have that worry of physical wealth and other ties that you have in your physical society.

~

The following views were conveyed by a spirit identified as the 12th Viscount. This spirit had visited the Circle to converse about their role when assisting some spirits to cross over to the Light from their state of being earthbound at an unspecified location since the 17th-century.

Qn: Would you let us know your name?
Visitor: 12th Viscount... [53]

Qn: Viscount, where did you first join us?
Viscount: Castle gates. There was much to do. The trying[54] of the Actuaries was a bit of a challenge, don't you know. There were many that went on to the Light but pray you will understand in good time. There are many things that require love at this level, and there are many coming to the reality of a better existence and life should they wish to join those in the lighted Realms where the Creators love envelopes one and all.

Qn: Have you come from the Light, Viscount? (Yes). Did you join at the castle gates to help collect others that needed to go to the Light? (Yes). The Universe is dark, how is the Light created in the spirit world?
Viscount: It is the light of the Creator's or God's energy, imagine a field of plants which many exist within. If you need an example, take your books of pictures, they are not real solid pictures; they are light created by energy, it is electrical in that instance, but the Creator's energy lights your own land beyond this planet's surface.

---

53 Part of the name given was unintelligible.
54 Actuaries are insurance and/or financial risk assessors. I did not ask what that trying problem was, but maybe it was something to do with Actuaries weighing up something rather than the passing of criminal judgements.

Qn: When a spirit is ready to leave its physical body, they are told to look out for the Light. (Yes). What is that Light?
Viscount: It is a doorway to the higher realms.

Qn: But the Universe is dark.
Viscount: Your physical Universe is dark to your eyes, but it is not devoid of energy and with the right equipment you would see some of what you think is black and empty, but it is not.

Qn: Are spirits bright? (Yes). The more spirits there are, the brighter the light. (Yes). Is that why they come together to form communities? (Yes). Can you clarify that please?
Viscount: Not sure what you are asking.

Qn: OK, I once saw a huge dome of light, and it seemed that its light was being radiated from the bright white silhouettes of people lining the base of this dome; there were many silhouettes of people standing in rows and behind them there were buildings in rows like a city skyline. What was I seeing[55].
Viscount: The welcome funnel to the Light

Qn: Is a welcome funnel what you go through when you go through to the Light? (Yes). Did I go through then?
Viscount: No, nearly. You would not be allowed to stay.

Qn: Are there other spirits here in the room waiting to go into the Light?

---

55   The individual asking this question was explaining an experience they had whilst under anaesthesia during an operation. They experienced being drawn towards a huge dome of bright light. As they drew closer to this dome, they saw lines of bright white silhouettes of human shapes in front of what appeared to be a brightly lit city skyline, before suddenly experiencing a 'whooshing' sensation of being pulled backwards following which they regained consciousness from the operation.

Viscount: No, you saw them through as you went along on your travels.

Qn: *When spirits stay around the physical Earth for years, but then eventually see Light, what do they see?*
Viscount: They see the same. It can just be a simple thing to remove them from living in such a small space.

Qn: *How important is the Light to the spirit world?*
Viscount: It is important to all the world. It is the birthplace of creation. It is the life of all the world and Universe surrounding you. Without its energy directing things, then life would cease to exist. In fact, it would never have been created.

Qn: *Have you told us about your own experience of the Light?* (Yes).

The next transcript details a challenging conversation held with a young boy who seemed to be illiterate and had not passed into the Light at the time of his death. His personal experience and recollections had to be conveyed through a spirit Guide. Shortly after the conclusion of this conversation he was able to cross over into the Light.

Qn: *Good evening. Who is visiting us?*
(The new visitor spent their time drawing a rectangle, circle, triangle, square, cloud, tree. Then a bigger circle, a cartwheel with spokes, and a cart with wheels).

Qn: *You're getting good at this, who are you?* (No response). *Are you drawing a house with clouds, do the shapes all come together to form a house?* (No response). *Do you wish to talk about a house with clouds*

in the sky, and a cart with wheels. (Yes). Did an animal pull the cart? (Yes). Was it a horse? (Yes). Did you live in England? (No response). America? (No response). Did you live in Scotland?
Visitor: Yes, by water.

Qn: Are you a lady? (No response). Are you a gentleman? (No response). Are you a girl? (No response). Are you a boy? (Yes). You are a boy; did you wear a kilt? (Yes). Did you use it to wrap yourself in at night when you slept? (Yes). Did you live with your family? (Yes). Did you go to school? (No response). Did you learn lots from your family? (Yes). Did you live on a farm? (No response). Did you live on a Croft?[56] (Yes). Did your family have any animals? (Yes). Did they have cows? (No response). Did they have sheep? (Yes). Did they have chickens? (Yes). Did you meet up with your family there. (Yes). Would you like to tell us how old you were? (10). Who brought you here?
Visitor: Someone standing beside you.

Qn: Is somebody beside me helping you? (Yes). Is it a lady?
Visitor: No, name is John.

Qn: Did you meet John recently? (Yes). Did you meet John while travelling near your home.
Visitor: Flodden Field.[57]

Qn: Did you march with your dad? (No response). Did you march with your family? (Yes). Did you go to the Light very recently, like

---

56 A small, rented farm or plot of arable land in Scotland.

57 History records show that Flodden field was the scene of one of the largest battles fought between the English and an invading Scottish army in Northumbia in 1513.

yesterday? *(Yes). And John has brought you back. (Yes). Can you tell me what it was like when you went to the Light?*
Visitor: Good. The people looked after me. I found that I could not get over everything. The atmosphere…

Qn: That's your word isn't it, John? (Yes). His words only, if possible, please.
Visitor:… the feeling of cuddling and it melted away all heartache and pain, and I felt renewed like I had risen, lifted up, and I felt that I was ready to move forward into this new home and with life to myself again.

Qn: What were you doing before you went into the Light?
Visitor: Waiting in limbo. Neither belonging nor feeling belonged to. It was not really an existence of life, just passing time venturing around looking for purpose and meaning and understanding.

Qn: John is putting words into what he is saying. The boy is saying 'knowing'. Did you go to Light recently? (Yes). What colour is your hair? (Red). Were you with me yesterday? (Yes). Were you upset? (Yes). Why?
Visitor: There was so much sadness, and it was unnecessary.

On two other separate occasions we were visited by two spirits who introduced themselves as Clara and Yvonne. This is what they had to say about their experiences and existence in the Light.

Clara

Qn: Would you like to give us your name? (Clara). Have you visited here before. (No). Have you been into the Light yet? (Yes).

Well, tell us a little bit about yourself and where you lived.
Clara: A round house.

Qn: A long time ago? (Yes). Was that England? (Yes). Perhaps you'd just like to tell us why the Light was so special for you? (Love). What do you do in the Light?
Clara: I live and exist.

Qn: Do you talk with other people?
Clara: Yes. I came from the Scottish Isles.

Qn: You have said that you live and exist, but how do you live?
Clara: Like you do here.

Qn: You live in a house? (Yes). You have neighbours? (Yes). What sort of house do you live in?
Clara: A double-fronted house. It has two rounds.

Qn: Do you share the house?
Clara: With my family.

Qn: Are these adults?
Clara: And children.

Qn: Will these children grow up and leave home?
Clara: If they choose.

Qn: So, what you're saying is, that a child can choose to stay as a child in the Light?
Clara: Yes. All children are rebellious. Some develop really slowly.

Qn: Are you saying that an individual can pass over as elderly but may choose to be a child in spirit?

Clara: Yes, they can do that. You can reach old age here but still be a very young spirit.

Qn: Apart from meeting with family and friends, is there anything else you like to do?
Clara: Read, live and exist.

Qn: Do you go anywhere?
Clara: Yes, meetings and to the lodge for discussion and learning.

Qn: Have you aged in spirit?
Clara: Yes. Not a lot. Time is different.

Qn: Do you look different? (Yes). How can you look different?
Clara: You can choose how you look in the energy.

Yvonne

Qn: Will you share your name and who you are please?
Yvonne: Yvonne. I am a woman of a certain age and nationality. I am from Scotland, and I migrated south, like the birds. This is when I met my husband, and we had a family of three children. I am pleased to report that they are all wearing well both in this world and yours.

Qn: Were you a lady of leisure?
Yvonne: I was employed during the war. I am an expert at what I did, I would make things as were required by our men.

Qn: What did you make during the war?
Yvonne: Top secret munitions during the second war.

Qn: Who invited you to visit this evening?
Yvonne: I was sent by an old friend of yours. He has not yet fully got

to grips with it all. He will come and talk to you himself one day. Hopefully not in the too distant future.

Qn: Can you talk about how you see spirit?
Yvonne: I see my new world.

Qn: Have you been in spirit long?
Yvonne: All on and off.

Qn: What do you mean by that please?
Yvonne: I have had many physical lives, and I can exist here between them, so on and off.

Qn: If you were to describe energy. How would you describe it?
Yvonne: It depends on what dimension you are in.

Qn: When you refer to a dimension, are you talking about the layers of spirit?
Yvonne: This is but one layer.

Qn: I am aware there are many layers, and different levels of vibration. Can you describe the Level that you are at and what the energy is to you?
Yvonne: It is life. It is all embracing because it forms our existence, at all Levels.

Qn: How does a simple piece of rock feel to you?
Yvonne: On which plane?

Qn: Your plane.
Yvonne: Like a rock.

Qn: If you were to go down a Level, how would you describe it?
Yvonne: A piece of rock.

Qn: You can see that rock. (Yes). You can feel that rock. (Yes). If you pushed your energy into the rock, could you do that? (Yes). I'm not asking you to do it, but can you merge with rock?
Yvonne: No. Too slow.

Qn: Can you merge or blend with a spirit on a higher Level than you are?
Yvonne: Only if they match my frequency of vibration.

Qn: Are you able to blend with all spirits on your Level?
Yvonne: Those that choose to blend with me, and only those that I choose in return.

Qn: When you blend with another spirit, does that become permanent?
Yvonne: No, you can blend for as long as the agreement is mutual.

Qn: What is the purpose of blending?
Yvonne: To feel each other on an intimate level. It is a merging of mind and body.

Qn: When you go back to your Level, are you going to see other spirits on a regular basis?
Yvonne: Yes, in the same way that you meet each other, I see them. You see with this dimension's eyes I see other dimensions.

A short message from Doris

Qn: How would you describe being in the Light.
Doris: I would say it is not as hard as it was on this physical body in this time. I would say that the Light goes on in love and happiness.

The higher the operation the nearer to the Creator. You learn the more peaceful you become, and that brings a sereneness to your life and existence. You cannot grasp it now; your minds are too restricted. There is an infinite possibility of outcomes and, as you are aware, you can make your own choices in how your life in the physical also applies to the spiritual.

❧

Finally, this short conversation with Alicia, currently working as an apprentice Guide with the writer, she had crossed to the Light after having spent a few years in an earthbound state.

Qn: Hello Alicia. Will you say a few words about your own passing to spirit.
Alicia: I danced for so long it became second nature to me even after I passed. Then I found you again and went into the Light[58]. This meant I could return to learn and practice being a Guide. It is an amazing job, filled with emotion for the good and bad times of your subject. You cannot let your emotions rule though.

Qn: Have you been a Guide for a long time?
Alicia: No. Only for you.

Qn: Have you learned a lot? (Yes). Am I trying subject to work with?
Alicia: Yes. All humans are, I think.

Qn: Were you surprised all those years ago when we first visited the other Circle demonstration? (No). What gave cause for you to follow?

---

58   This was the first time that I had understood, despite the many conversations we had with Alicia, that she had previously been earthbound and had entered the Light just prior to becoming an apprentice Guide.

Alicia: A Medium's light. When she visited and danced with us, I knew that I had to follow. Then when I saw Sergei, I knew I was in the right place.

Qn: Had you been a little bit lost. (Yes). Are you happy where you are? (Yes). Has it given you a future to look forward to?
Alicia: Yes. I have my freedom to live, love, and dance, and when I please.

֎

While exploring the concept and importance of the Light, some individuals on social media may have been misled into believing that entering the Light will immediately result in their newly liberated spirit undergoing another cycle of physical rebirth and regeneration. Conversely, it has also been suggested that by rejecting the Light the newly liberated spirit will have the freedom to explore and exist within the Universe as it may desire. I do not typically engage with social media. Neither am I inclined to dispute such claims for accuracy or claim to have definitive answers to the assertions that have been made on social media. However, I am fortunate to have had the opportunity to pose these questions directly to visiting spirits and so I invited the Chief to provide some clarification of those claims. Please note that this conversation pertains to the newly liberated spirit of an individual immediately after their physical death, rather than an ongoing existence in the physical realm.

Qn: Some people have been discussing on social media that when a person goes into the Light, they will go straight into a rebirth and regeneration process. Is this correct? (Yes). Does the person have the choice to go into this process, or can they exist within the Light within one of the various dimensions or Levels? (Yes). It has also been said

that by turning their back on the Light, the person will have the Universe at their disposal and can enter any Level that they may have originally come from. (Yes). So, if it doesn't matter whether a person crosses over to the Light, what is better to do?
Chief: Go into the Light.

Qn: Can you regenerate outside the Light and be reborn in the physical again outside the Light? (No). Is it correct that if you stay outside the Light, you can travel around as far as you want to go? (Yes). Will you be alone? (Yes). If you go into the Light, will you be with friends and family? (Yes). Can you remain in the Light without needing to go into the rebirth process? (Yes). And still be able to explore the Universe. (Yes). And move between the Levels in the Light.
Chief: Yes, but only from the Level you are in, downwards.

Qn: Can you go into the Light and come back out again as you may wish? (Yes). Can you travel on the Earth Level if you come out of the Light as much as you want to as a spirit. (Yes). Do you have to go into the Light first to do these things. (Yes). After entering the Light and after what you see in the Light, will it be your own choice whether to come out again. (Yes).

Qn: If people don't follow the advice to go into the Light, is that a problem for the spirit realm?
Chief: It means they will wander the Earth plane forever until their energy shadows. It is not ideal; they will attach themselves to a living target and either gain energy from the target or try to become that target's existence.

❧

As if to make a substantive point, a spirit identifying as Jenny then immediately arrived to share and demonstrate her own experience existing in the Light.

Qn: Who do we have visiting now? Can you tell us about yourself please.
Jenny: I am Jenny Longbottom from Syracuse in the States of America.

Qn: Could you tell us a bit about yourself?
Jenny: I am woman. I am 37 of years. I am living longer but prefer 36 or 37 years. I come with my faithful pet wolf and, like you, this is my companion. I think you have a question.

Qn: Have you been to the Light? (Yes). Do you still live in the Light? (Yes). Why do you prefer to live in the Light rather than on the plane?
Jenny: The love of the Creator engulfs you in the Light and all your worries disperse. On the Earth Level you can still feel the hurt and high pain, the anger, and love of those around you.

Qn: Living in the Light, would you be forced to be reborn in the physical again?
Jenny: If it was required, you would be asked. You do not have to, but would you deny the Creator. I have not been asked, neither have my parents nor grandparents.

Qn: Apart from the Creator, who would ask you to be reborn on the Earth plane again?
Jenny: His Messengers.

Qn: Is there a group or organisation that oversights this?
Jenny: Of course. It would be chaos otherwise.

Qn: Does this organisation send a Messenger to you? (Yes). Are you permitted to decide whether that's what you want to do. (Yes). Did someone contact you to come here to speak with us? (Yes). Is that someone a First Nation American? (Yes). Is his name CP? (Yes).

How did he contact you about speaking with this Circle?
Jenny: He sent out a request via the angel attached to your Circle Leader, she selected myself.

Qn: So, in that short space of time (no more than 10 minutes had passed) *the message was sent out and CP received several responses.* (Yes). *And he was able to select you.*
Jenny: No, the angel did who is attached to the Circle Leader.

Qn: Who is the angel?
Jenny: She wishes to keep her anonymity.

⁓

The Chief's comments have offered deeper clarity on the subject without entirely disregarding the social media statements. The primary message remains – newly liberated spirits are encouraged to enter and explore the Light before making it their decision not to enter – no harm in trying first. Maybe some messages from spirits are not always fully understood or being inaccurately conveyed. In Jenny's case it seems neither she nor her parents or grandparents have been asked to return to the physical after entering the Light and she appears to be quite happy there along with her family who have existed there for probably three generations. You can read more conversations connected to this topic in the Sections titled 'Transitioning between Worlds' and 'Earthbound Spirits'.

I could not resist asking one question related to the use of social media. This was answered by the Conglomerate, who then went into a little more detail than I expected.

Qn: What will happen if individuals return to the Light with social media?

Conglomerate: The one thing, my friend, they will learn to do without is social media. We have not got that yet and let's hope we never do. It is not necessary. Why do you need social media when you only have to think of somebody, and you can go and visit them? It is not like you are trying to communicate with your families, who are many miles away or even across continents. You can do it. There are no restrictions. You can visit. You don't have to rely on social media. You can live your lives in the areas where you have decided to designate your hometown. You can live there with others, the same as in the physical, but there is a big difference. There is no fear. There is no violence. There is peace, harmony, love. People appreciate each other. You mix within your Level and below, so you choose where you wish to be in your society. You do not want the aggravation; you do not want any more of this negativity that you experience in the physical. Ever learning and happy.

Remember, time is not the same in spirit as it is in the physical where time accelerates because you measure it by the day. In spirit, time is not measured by the day. There is no need to measure it by the day, it is measured by the people that return home. They will be welcomed home after they have passed from physical. "It is wonderful to see you. I have been missing you, I think for a while it is good that you are here, now come join us". A big celebration will go on for quite a while. It is an evolving thing and brings in new people. You must talk. You must tell. You have to say what has happened. Tell more of your life. Story telling is still a big thing. People tell of their experiences. They enthuse within their family group and their friends. "What have you still been doing?", "Well, I had two grandchildren before I came up, just like you, Grandma, and they are bundles of fun". The story goes on.

You wondered what they did when they went back to spirit, didn't you? This may give you a bit of an idea. A celebration of others' lives, but not in the celebratory way you have in the physical, where you remember with photos. In spirit, it's calm. Let us know all what has happened to you since we last saw you. Then we tell them what we have been up to. But of course, the time difference means that they have crammed more into that time than we have. Then of course you have the great speakers, when they come the great speakers give talks. They tell us what has happened, what are the newest developments, how they feel, have they searched their heart.

There is Plato, he still comes and talks to people. There are still many of the great that come and give their thoughts and their passions to those that will listen. There are those that decide that they wish to go down again because they wish to get rid of some of the karma or memories that they have not yet fulfilled, and they take back what they have heard. Alright, they take it back in the subconscious. So, there is some rudimentary knowledge of what has been said and what they have heard the great speakers speak about in the different halls, libraries and areas designated for this around the spirit world.

Transitioning between Worlds

Have you ever thought about what happens after death? For individuals who adhere to the belief in an eternal afterlife within the spiritual realm, it is pertinent to explore questions regarding how the spirit transitions from the physical body and the subsequent experiences it may encounter. Perhaps your perspectives have been shaped by portrayals you have seen in films or on television. For those individuals who have an interest in understanding what happened immediately following the end of a physical existence, this Section details some extracts from several conversations with spirits about this event and provides a little insight into the process by which the spirit departs from an individual's physical body. From the answers given, I also became intrigued by the process that might occur when a spirit energy is reborn into a physical body.

    I fully acknowledge that some individuals might still find it challenging to believe in the notion that we all exist as an eternal spiritual energy that can be called upon to enter a new, developing physical body at any given time, and that upon inhabiting this newly formed physical body we must remain there until its natural life concludes. A life cycle which may start over only with the individual spirit's consent. Given the potential regularity of this life cycle, it is reasonable to assume there must be an organised process within the spiritual realm to facilitate these recurrent, almost cyclic, occurrences.

    We had established a good understanding with the spirit Guides on other subjects, so it was time to ask whether they would be willing to provide insight into the processes involved when the spirit energy transitions between physical and spirit worlds. By transitioning, I am referring to the movement of the spirit energy between the physical and spiritual states and vice versa. It is the process that is often described by some as incarnation or reincarnation. It is important to understand that each occurrence of physical reincarnation involves merging into a different physical body with a memory that starts afresh, whilst the memory of the spirit energy remains unchanged and stored in a higher conscious.

Earlier discussions with spirits had already provided us with valuable insights into the process for when a life moves into the Light, I thought it would be interesting to have ordinary spirits also share their experiences and memories of how they left their physical body at the time of their physical death.

Transitioning from a Physical Life back to Spirit

Qn: What happens when an individual passes from a physical body to spirit?

Chief: I will talk about how life transforms from this physical world to the next. When you have come to the end of use for your incarnate body, you transform to the next level of existence[59]. Your energy is passed from your physical body; it seeps out through the gaps in your body. These are miniscule to your eye, but so is your energy component.

When you release your energy, you will still feel like yourself, you will feel light, you will be able to move with ease. Life as you

---

59 Leaving a physical body is not just about crossing over to the Light, it is also about reaching the next level of your spiritual existence. This may depend on whether you had attained the path that had been set, whether you had learned new things, and whether your behaviour was sufficient to raise your spiritual vibration to a higher level.

knew it before will have ceased to exist except in your memories, these you carry with you so the awareness of who you have been will not be lost. You carry the essence of yourself and your development with you. This is a crucial time, and those that love you will help to guide you through this critical stage and see you on the new path. You will not suffer the trauma of being unable to move ahead, as trauma is not a good state to be in, so we try to make the transition as easily for you as possible.

You will be met by people that you know. This will allow your physical body to be shed and your spirit to slowly ascertain the vibration level that it should be at. We call this the acclimatisation time; it is not instantaneous.

Qn: You mentioned about an energy component. Could you clarify that please.
Chief: Component is the energy that makes up an item.

Qn: Are you suggesting it is a component of anything?
Chief: No. Each component is made up of energy, how tightly depends on what it is. To move out you need to be able to pass through the body's component energy[60].

Qn: When the energy has left a physical body, what form does it take immediately when it comes back together?
Chief: It becomes a higher vibrating energy.

Qn: When the energy has left a physical body, does it form back into a physical shape.
Chief: Yes, at first. It then takes on the shape it desires. But you must

---

60 The physical body consists of a slower vibrating energy, and because it is vibrating at the same frequency our surroundings, existence appears solid to us.

remember your energy has been moulded by the body it has sat in for so long. Your energy fills the whole of your living body; it does not stop at your legs for example.

Qn: The fact that energy is held in the shape of the physical body until the individual learns to control the energy, does it stay that way? Is it like being reborn?
Chief: Yes, but it tends to be less painful than physical birth.

Qn: When an individual has left a physical body, what will happen to them in spirit after a week or so?
Chief: That all depends on what they have been led to expect.

Qn: If an individual were an atheist without belief, are they going to be stuck not expecting anything?
Chief: Yes. Usually, they may have been exposed to the idea of spirit. It is difficult nowadays to find a true atheist. They do get such a surprise.

Qn: Is there a lot of preparation going on when an individual is getting near to their passing.
Chief: Yes. There is the gathering.

Qn: Do their Guides have to prepare?
Chief: The word goes out. Also, those that are close will begin keeping an eye out.

Qn: When an individual has passed, and has been met, they may have concern for loved ones that might give cause for them to want to remain earthbound. Is it more important for them to go straight to the Light?
Chief: Yes ideally, and they may then be allowed to come straight back.

Qn: Do some not go to the Light so they can stay with their relatives for a few weeks? (Yes). Will they still have the time to go to the Light?
Chief: Yes. Time is always available to go to the Light.

Qn: Some people might decide to go straight to the Light and might not want to come back. (Yes). If an individual is getting very near to passing, who will be with them for their last few days?
Chief: Their Guides and their main family member, a mum, husband, etc. Sometimes a dog or cat.[61]

Qn: A little curiosity. You say that an individual will be met by spirit Guides and family. (Yes). What if they are all at different Levels in Spirit.
Chief: Above can come down. Down cannot go up.

Qn: What happens if a family member is of a lower vibration level to the individual who has passed, how will they be able to be greeted?
Chief: The individual who has passed will always enter at the lower vibration level at first.

Qn: Does this give time for them to meet again, and does the individual have to decide whether to continue with their own progression to a higher vibration level? (Yes). Is there anyone else present who must be there?
Chief: Yes, the Recorder[62] to keep a check that all has proceeded as planned.

---

61   When a physical body dies the spirit energy leaving that body may be in a state of shock or possesses little or no understanding/knowledge of what happens next – this is why it is necessary for the released spirit to be met by spiritual Guides, family and friends to welcome and help their transition back to their life in spirit.

62   The Recorder appears to be one of several different official roles there are in the spirit world. These spirits have the task of keeping a record of those spirits transitioning from the physical to back to spirit.

Qn: Will disabled people have problems crossing over to the Light, or do they take their disability with them?

Conglomerate: No, only for a short time until they realise that they no longer have their disability. It is not instantaneous; they do not go out and suddenly throw their wheelchairs or crutches away. They will still be conditioned to the situation immediately after they pass but once they realise there are no spiritual disabilities, all is well[63].

Qn: How does an individual who has been blind all their life see the Light and transition back to spirit?

Conglomerate: We adjust the light; they may not understand how they are seeing it, but they will see it. As their vision becomes clearer, they will start to make out things in the Light. If they accept the Light, their relatives and friends will lead them gently by the arms into the Light and to them it will be just one step as usual. They will not be able to see suddenly because this would frighten them. If they have not been blinded all their physical life, there may be some vision there for them when they pass over and they may understand what they are seeing. But to take one who has never seen and subject them to instant sight would be too dramatic of a change. Some things will gradually come to them as they start to adapt and accept their new surroundings.

Qn: When a person leaves their physical body will they return to a basic vibration level in spirit, or return to the level they were at before entering the physical?

Conglomerate: You will return at a lower level, not necessarily the lowest level, it depends on who the person is, but you will not go

---

63 Later in this Section are the extracts from a conversation with a spirit identifying herself as Half Moon. She had suffered with a disability during her physical life, and she briefly speaks about her experience of what happened to her after she passed to spirit.

straight into the upper Levels; the change would be too much and the vibration level needs to gradually rebuild. This does not mean that you will be inhibited in what you can do within the area at that point in time, for you will have those around you to enjoy again to celebrate and rejoice in their company.

Qn: Is it an energy fog and different densities for different levels?
Conglomerate: It is like a line where when you reach this level of vibration you are within a band. But to cross through the Veil, as you might call it, you must attain the right vibration level that will let you pass through it into the next Level. You cannot just go through. The Veil is a good description.[64]

Qn: As you might say, everything else vibrating at a different level disappears and it is almost as though you are going through a Veil?
Conglomerate: You understand why we feel that Veil is a good description. The next Level becomes visible to you when you go through, and the other Level will disappear from your view.

Qn: Are there spirits that can go through all these Veils just by adjusting their energy?
Conglomerate: There are special spirits. You can always travel downwards but not stay too long unless you have a particular allotted task. But you cannot travel upwards.

Qn: How does an individual's memory return?
Conglomerate: It is as easy as opening a door. Not straight away, it will be too overwhelming for you. First, you must adjust to the fact

---

64 The use of Veil as a descriptive word for passing to spirit or moving between the spirit Levels has been used many times. Try to imagine your current surroundings slowly disappearing and being visually replaced by the new surroundings of the next Level or dimension.

you have gone from a physical body back to spirit, and you would find it too much to have that memory all poured straight back in. So, it is opened slowly, a strand at a time the little door is opened.

Qn: Would a person have to sum up their life on Earth first?
Conglomerate: Yes, your understanding of what you have learned, and a summing up of what you have obtained and has been achieved. It would not be good for you to have all this information before you are able to digest the information.

Qn: After physical death is the residue energy always kept as one, or can it be split up and distributed.
Conglomerate: By residue energy, I do not understand.

Qn: The energy of the spirit rather than residue energy of the physical body when we die on this Earth plane.
Conglomerate: We are the whole spirit.

Qn: Is it kept as one or can it be distributed?
Conglomerate: It is kept as one for that is your identity, your personality. It is your physical body that will disintegrate and return as the natural residue energy to the ground, but your spirit energy will stay as one for it will be you and you will be welcomed into the world of spirit as you are. For natural energy, expect to know that the physical body will feed others.

☙

Following on from the answers provided by the Chief and the Conglomerate, the Circle received further accounts from spirits who shared their recollections of what immediately occurred after leaving their physical body. The first account was provided by a spirit who chose to remain anonymous. By the end of the visit, it had become apparent that this spirit had passed a long time ago. As is often the case, it can be challenging for spirits to discuss time as they typically lack an accurate sense of time. This often made it difficult to make accurate judgement on dates and highlights the differences there are in the perception of time between the physical and spiritual dimensions[65].

Qn: ... Are you a visitor? (Yes). Is this your first visit? (Yes). Are you here for a purpose? (Yes). What is that purpose?
Visitor: To tell how it is.

Qn: Would you like to do that then? (No response). Can you tell us what you know about being in spirit?
Visitor: You wanted to know about passing experiences.

Qn: Are you here to talk about your own experience of passing? (Yes). Well, please tell us what happened.
Visitor: I died.

Qn: What happened immediately after you died?
Visitor: I was above myself; I found that I could see there was nothing around me. There appeared to me a light and it shone to me. I became aware of the shadows of people around me. They became stronger than the surroundings of my physical body[66], they eclipsed this image, and I found myself in the company of friends and strangers that I felt ease with. I walked with them, then the Light and love grew stronger the further I accompanied them into the area[67]. I was

---

65 In the spirit world time is infinite.

66 This spirit is describing their experience of passing through the Veil – their own description for the moment that their vibration started to increase as they left their physical body.

67 The spirit is recollecting their walk into the Light.

surprised that I was greeted with such love and celebration. I was helped to adjust into this new, but old and familiar environment.

Qn: Were strangers there? (Yes). Did those strangers introduce themselves to you? (Yes). Who were they?
Visitor: My Guides. That was why they seemed familiar, I now know.

Qn: Was there someone who looked like an official? (Yes). Would you be able to tell me who that might have been?
Visitor: He confirmed all my details and helped me define my walk into the spirit world[68].

Qn: Was he carrying anything. (Yes). Could you tell me what it was? (Book). Was he writing in those books? (Yes). How would you describe being in spirit?
Visitor: Better than being in the physical. You want for nothing as you need nothing. Just a pleasant existence.

Qn: Where in your spirit existence do you now live?
Visitor: With my partner of many years. I walked adrift for a while, my body[69] following my dreams. I then met the love of my existence, and we comfort, support, and love one another.

Qn: Do you have any eyes?
Visitor: Yes, not like yours are physically. These work on a different level, and they work perfectly[70].

---

68 This a reference to the attendance of a 'Recorder' who is assigned to manage the upkeep of records within the spirit world.

69 This spirit is referring to their new existence in spirit.

70 For anyone who may have concern about 'sight' in spirit, the Chief provided this reassuring message to one of the Circle members:
"Chief: We still have eyes you know; they just see differently. They are not made of flesh, as you know, and they do not have cones and rods. ☛

Qn: When you were met by others after your passing, did they address you by your physical name? (Yes). *Has your physical name changed in the spirit world.* (Yes). *How long did it take for that to happen?*
Visitor: I have no idea; time is not recorded in the way you do here.

Qn: Do you have any pets around you?
Visitor: Animals choose you rather than in the physical where you sometimes choose the animal[71].

Qn: Who are you?
Visitor: I grew up on a farm in rural Scotland. Life was hard but we were safe till the English Wars.

Qn: Can you tell us your name?
Visitor: No. you will find out when you cross. It will be my pleasure to meet you then.

◆

The mother of a Circle member, who had passed away two years before, frequently visited to communicate with her family from the spirit realm. During one of her visits, I took the opportunity to inquire about what she could recollect about her own passing.

Qn: Would you be prepared to explain what happened just after your passing?
JMum: Do you mean when I died?

They are energy on a different level, and they do not need the trappings of this physical Level."

71 This is an interesting statement to have made and had not been asked about – that animal spirits are free and choose whom they wish to accompany.

Qn: *Just after you died, it was probably my singing.*
JMum: You have Welsh in you. We are all good singers, if not wear ear plugs.

Qn: *So, what happened?*
JMum: I did not feel pain or panic. I felt good. I could see you all, but I was not worried. A little, gentle confusion. Then I saw my parents, family and friends come to the front of a colourful light, I was torn for a second as to whether to stay or go to them. But the love coming from them wrapped around me, and as I moved towards them, I became aware of a stronger feeling of this being right, and became aware of others walking beside me and I entered into the Light and was greeted by them. I saw that you had all faded behind me, for now [72].

Qn: *The people that walked beside you, were they your Guides?*
JMum: I found out later they were. Which is why they felt safe and familiar.

Qn: *Just before you passed, were you knowledgeable of spirit?*
JMum: Only from the Church. Jesus said to the thief beside him, 'today you will be in my father's house'; they missed his most important words to date [73].

Qn: *Were you surprised when the physical world disappeared? (Yes). Were you fearful?*
JMum: No. It felt right and the love is exceptional.

---

72 Another interpretation of passing through the Veil and crossing over into the Light, that also covers how she now travels in and out of the Light as she so wishes to visit and speak with her family.

73 I admit to unfamiliarity with this statement, but I was told that JMum was of traditional Welsh church faith and was re-emphasising that when you pass you can go to the heaven of your own belief..

Qn: You do not have to answer this question. When you passed and you left your body. What were you wearing in spirit as your energy reformed?
JMum: My same clothes. I took their energy with me.

༄

A woman who lived with a disability throughout her physical life shared her experiences and recollections with the Circle. At one point, she seemed to reflect on her physical life before passing. She identified herself as Half Moon.

Qn: Can you tell us who you are, please.
Visitor: I am Half Moon.

Qn: Are you a First Nation visitor? (No). Do you come from the Far East?
Half Moon: Yes, I am from China. My name is Half Moon. I was born under the moonlight of a half-moon.

I am looking at my physical self. My robe is of red silk. I am privileged to have a home and servants. I am still fairly young. I passed when I was in my 30's. I felt that you would appreciate my talking to you.

I was not belonging to anyone as I had a disability on Earth that plagued my life and ended it early, hence I had no soul mate. Then I found my soul mate when I went home.[74] I still go to visit my homeland every now and then, but so much of it is unrecognisable to me now.

---

74 Half Moon is referring to how she found her soul mate when she returned to the spirit world and can travel between the physical Earth and the Light at her own leisure.

Qn: When you passed over, did you take your own life? (No). Did the disability take your life? (Yes). Did you go straight to the Light? (Yes). What happened?
Half Moon: I can tell you that there was still my disability for a while afterwards but then, like getting better, it slowly disappeared.

Qn: Did you go through any process for your physical disability to disappear when you passed to spirit?
Half Moon: I had to settle and adjust[75].

Qn: Were you helped by others? (Yes). Could you tell me how they helped you?
Half Moon: They comforted and guided me through settlement.

Qn: Did you know these people? (Yes). Did you know them from the physical? (No). Did you know them previously in spirit? (No response).

∞

The recurrent message underscores the importance of trusting family, friends, or spiritual Guides who may be present at an individual's passing. These spirits are there to welcome and assist the individual with their transition back to the spirit realm.

I had been unable to transcribe the conversation from a visit by a close friend whose spirit visited the Circle literally a week after his passing. However, I recollect his comments about feeling disoriented in his new surroundings and being somewhat confused about the absence of any need for food, drink, or sleep. He had also mentioned that he was being cared

---

[75] This seems to be part of a process that most returning to spirit will go through.

for by his parents. It seems that some initial disorientation following a transition to spirit may be common, but that it remains important for individuals to embrace the change and to transition to the Light as promptly as possible.

In addition to friends, family and Guides being present at the time an individual leaves their physical body, I was curious about the spirit who is present and has been reported to have been making notes in a book.

Qn: Hello, would you like to introduce yourself please?
Visitor: Yes, I am Sydney, and you can call me a Witness.

Qn: Can you tell me what you do?
Sydney: I come from the Hall of Life Records. I come to observe and note the date one returns to one's life eternal.

Qn: So, you attend to every person that passes back into spirit.
Sydney: No, I could not possibly do that. I have an allocation to uphold and see through and record.

Qn: What are you recording, or how do you do it?
Sydney: Just the last page of their book of life. Date, time and reason.

Qn: Are you part of the process of people returning to spirit? (Yes). So, you must be there at the time of their passing? (Yes). What about those who go from spirit to physical.
Sydney: That is already in their book. That is preordained. Although accidents can occur during that time and the start may need to be tweaked and rearranged.

Qn: If you are there with family, friends and Guides to meet somebody but they refuse to go into the Light. What do you have to do?

Sydney: Nothing. If they refuse to see the Light, I can only record the details in the book.

Qn: *So somewhere in the records of the Hall of Life, there are gaps for those spirits who have not come back.*
Sydney: No, the volume is complete. It is just you are already back in spirit; it is just you have not found your way home yet.

Qn: *Would it be better to get each of those coming back to countersign their book?*
Sydney: It is only truth that is written.

Transitioning from Spirit into a Physical Life

Qn: *How is the memory cleared from a spirit prior to re-birth into a new physical body?*
Conglomerate: It is symbolic[76]. It is a symbolic process that you go through. It can be a drink[77] in most cases, depending of course upon your religion or outlook on life. For most, it is a symbolic drink where the memories are separated. It is no good going down to the Earth full of all the memories that you have in your possession from when you are in spirit. It is too much for you to handle, so we separate, we cause... a block, that is the perfect word, a block so that these memories are kept here[78]. We refer to that as your higher self-

---

76 The Conglomerate is identifying the removal of the spirit memory as a symbolic act that occurs through a personal act taken by the individual spirit rather than as an act of unexpected and sudden memory loss. It becomes the individual spirit's own voluntary act. This may differ for everyone and depend upon personal choice.

77 Although spirits need neither food nor drink to sustain their energy, there had been many references by spirits using energy to recreate tastes and smells from past physical lives to re-enact favourite pastimes from their time on Earth.

78 The Conglomerate is referring to the higher self-conscious or higher

conscious, that is still working, still acknowledging, still operating; it does not die. We do not kill off your memories or remove them, that part of your psyche, that part of your knowledge is still operational.

So, you may talk to your higher self-conscious, and your higher self-conscious may talk to you. But it is not for the higher self-conscious to pass down knowledge to you. It is stored for you so that it is there when you require it when you return home to Spirit. So, spirit cause a blockage of information. I think that is an easy way to understand it; if you imagine a cable and part of the cable has all your memories in, and another part of the cable is the spirit that is active and ready to learn, and we put our little doorway right through the middle, then close the doorway and lock it.

Sometimes there is a little gap in the door or maybe the seal has not been as tight as we thought, and little factors seep through. That is where you get *Deja vu* moments, when you stand in a place you think you have been before? This is where information has slipped through that little gap. A distant memory triggered. It is symbolic to show your willingness for this to occur. So, you may be given a drink, you may be given a sacred fruit, it may be bread. It depends on your understanding of sacredness. This is the acceptance of the deed. It is saying I accept the situation, and then of course, you are ready to go down to Earth as a small babe with the ability to learn unhindered.

If you had come down with a certain task in mind to bring information for use in the physical world, then that will be tucked within a small amount of the psyche you have brought down to use, but it will not be released. Look on it as a slow-release tablet that works over a period, it will be slowly seeping into your conscious mind. The information then you will use, be it inspiration, be it knowledge, be it great heart, or a book that you write, it will be something that you are destined to do.

---

self which is addressed in the Section with the same title.

Qn: Would you explain how the energy gets into a physical body prior to its birth?
Chief: The same way as it seeps away when it leaves. Energy can become as small as required.

Qn: At what point in the period of a human pregnancy? (No response). After birth? (No). At some point during foetus development. (Yes). Any point in particular? (Varies). Can you give an example?
Chief: Twins. They go in together. This enables interaction to grow between them. Their energies blend to know each other before birth.

Qn: Is the period varied?
Chief: Yes. We need to know the physical baby is stable to a certain degree before energy enters.

Qn: Will others be present to help or watch the energy enter the baby's body?
Chief: Yes. With preparation before rebirth, then helping the energy into place. Also, the chord that attaches the spirit to its respective physical body needs to be attached.

Qn: Is the chord a special kind of energy. (Yes). Is it different from the energy that spirit is made up of?
Chief: No, just a different configuration. It is still a part of the spirit.

Qn: Does the chord just disappear?
Chief: It detaches from the body and is reabsorbed by the spirit[79].

Qn: Is the chord attached to any specific part of the body. (Yes). Could you disclose which part? (No).

---

79   This is a chord that connects the spirit energy with the physical body for the entirety of the physical life.

Based upon the answers provided, the process for a spirit to transition, or reincarnate, into a physical body is a little more complex to explain or understand. Two primary actions seem to be involved: the temporary removal of the spirit memory and the act of the selected spirit taking up the new identity of an unborn physical infant. Other additional steps may include determining who decides which spirit energy will return to the physical realm, when and for what purpose. The Circle was privileged to be visited by a spirit who did try to explain their experience of transitioning to physical birth.

Qn: ... Who are we talking to? ... You can write it on the table.
Visitor: I am about to talk to you on the subject of my physical birth. I climbed into my mother's womb, or rather my energy spark did. I adjusted to my new coat[80] then rested inside the warmth and safety of this cossetted place, becoming increasingly aware of the surrounding sounds both inside and outside my space. When I entered, my memory cleared of all my past expressions leaving me with just the basics for my survival.

Qn: Were you helped when you came down? (Yes). Who helped you?
Visitor: Helped by my team.

Qn: Do you mean your Guides? (Yes). Can you describe how they helped you, as you were an energy going into a physical body.
Visitor: They also kept me company while I waited to be born.

Qn: When was your memory removed?

---

80   The visiting spirit is referring to the physical body as a coat. Is it an energy spark that activates the physical heart rhythm?

Visitor: On entry. As my new body was opened to me, I entered through the vibrating cells and at this point all was emptied.

Qn: How was your spirit separated from the spirit of the mother?
Visitor: I was a separate entity.

Qn: You were kept separate from the other entity. (Yes). How long did you wait for your physical birth? (No response). OK, you had no concept of time? (No). Could your Spirit still move around freely? (No). Could you communicate with your Guides? (Yes). Obviously, a successful birth. (Yes). And did you enjoy that physical life?
Visitor: I had a job to do.

Qn: Did you make any contribution to physical?
Visitor: I like to think so.

※

The spirit visitor departed without revealing their name or any details about the physical existence they had been referring to at that time. This brief interaction offered further insight into understanding the transitioning discussions we had held with other spirits from various Levels. While the explanation provided is simplistic, the process may well be lengthier and more complex, rather than the reverse of transitioning back to spirit.

I did notice a small difference between what had been said by the Conglomerate and a visiting spirit on what happens at the point where the memory of the spirit is removed. The former identifies it as a symbolic event enacted by an action taken by the spirit, whilst the visitor seemed to be left in an instant with a memory limited to survival instinct, for that spirit was it a sudden event? However, as the Conglomerate had previously stated, it can also be an action of choice personally administered.

In all the many years that we had been sitting, only one spirit awaiting re-birth has visited our Circle. This happened just days before the final manuscript submission, prompting me to include the brief conversation we had. J is a young child who had been rescued from being an earthbound spirit over ten years ago and who frequently visited us to share how she was getting along in the Light. This is the transcript of that most recent conversation.

Qn: Someone new with us. Hello J, it's lovely to see you. Is all well now. (Yes). Are you happy? (Yes). Oh, you've got your Tiger back. (Yes). Oh, that's good. What happened to the Tiger?
J: Someone took.

Qn: How could that happen? Can you explain what happened?
J: I was not present.

Qn: So, your Tiger just disappeared. (Yes).

Qn: You've got your Tiger back. I can see it. He's looking after you. The little dog looks like a breed of sausage dog, isn't it? Is the little dog with you as well. (Yes). So, nobody's going to bother you now when you come to this Level, because the dog will have a go as well. When the Tiger is not there, the dog will be there?
J: Yes. The dog will alert the Tiger.

Qn: Were they given to you by the Lady? (Yes). Who do you live with now?
J: My family.

R: *Are you happy, J? (Yes). And you're allowed to come and visit us again? (Yes). Did you know the person that caused the problem. (Yes). So that's how they were able to cause the problem. (Yes). What are you planning to do in the future?*
J: Learning. I will be reborn soon and then I will grow quicker in understanding, and I will bring a message to the world.

Qn: *The world is interesting, J. I'm sure you'll be very good, and I hope you will be looked after really, really well. Do you know if you have a team picked out to look after you? (Yes). I hope they're special, for a special girl. Do you know where you are going to be born? (Yes). But you are not allowed to tell us, are you? (No). I hope it's a nice experience for you. Come and see us. (Yes). We'd love that and look forward to meeting you again sometime. Well, take care, my darling. Be safe. Love you. She's gone. In all these years that's the first time someone has come through to tell us they were going to be reborn.*

Qn: *Before J is reborn, is there a process that she has to go through? (Yes). What is that.*
Chief: She needs to assess what she needs or wants to fulfil.

Qn: *She's quite young. (Yes). Will she have choices in what she needs to learn in the physical?*
Chief: Yes. It's not going to be complicated. She has already experienced the loss and sadness. This time it will be different.

J was a very young spirit when she first entered what may have been her initial physical existence, possibly as an almost new spiritual energy. Unfortunately, it appears that her physical family was unable to care for her, leading to her abandonment at a shrine in a wooded area where her spirit was collected by an entity we came to know as the Lady. We learned that J began her new life in the Light with a new spiritual family, who looked after and loved her. The Lady permitted J to visit the Circle many times which helped to aid our understanding of how spirit children or new spiritual energies develop in the Light. J is now preparing for rebirth, and someone will be fortunate to welcome her.

Earthbound Spirits

When a spirit leaving its physical body at the time of an individual's death chooses not to walk into the Light or misses this opportunity for other reasons, it will become an earthbound spirit and risks being trapped on the physical Level (Earth plane) for an extended period. This spirit will likely stay on the physical Level until such time as they are rescued by other spirits or a spiritual Medium who possesses an ability to sense the presence of an earthbound spirit.

I wanted to understand the phenomenon of why some spirits, accidentally or by choice, become earthbound after departing their physical body. If the Light is as compelling and radiant as described, it raises the question of why a spirit might fail to perceive it or decide against following the guidance offered by family, friends, or spirit Guides who are present to assist the individual to return home. While it is probable that the spirit Guides may be unfamiliar to an individual, it is puzzling why the familiar faces of family and friends should be disregarded. For example, perhaps atheists perceive these apparitions as imaginary and therefore choose to ignore them due to their lack of belief in an afterlife, without realising they had already vacated their physical body.

Given the choice, I do not think that anyone should remain earthbound, it seems a lonely infinite existence. However, for whatever reasons, there are earthbound spirits and over the years, some earthbound spirits have visited the Circle asking for help to pass into the Light. While most spirits were willing to accept the help to cross quickly into the Light, some required encouragement and persuasion, perhaps due to ignorance and fear, but their crossing was always of their own free will. I sought to understand the reasons behind this phenomenon and invited some spirits to share their recollections. However, very few earthbound spirits were willing to discuss the circumstances they encountered.

Qn: Are earthbound spirits those who have not entered the Light. (Yes). Can you explain why spirits seem to have difficulty finding earthbound spirits and to help them go to the Light.
Chief: We can find them. They are just so focused on the physical, they can only see physical people.

Qn: Is it the physical person who sees the earthbound spirit, or is it the earthbound spirit who sees the physical person?
Chief: They see the physical person's light.[81]

Qn: When an earthbound spirit is attracted by this light of a person, do they follow it?
Chief: Yes. Sometimes we only need to distract them enough for them to see our light.

Qn: So, if an earthbound spirit can be distracted, what happens next?
Chief: It means we can collectively distract the earthbound spirit enough for them to register whoever we think can draw their attention. This will result in them usually crossing into the Light to become one in the Light with us all.

---

81 This is the spiritual light of our vibrating energy. It is something that cannot be seen by physical eyes, but spirits can see it. Some shine brighter than others and will depend on an individual's spiritual Level.

Qn: After the 'rescue' has taken place, does the earthbound spirit go to the Light. (Yes). Will they have to undergo any special process?
Chief: Yes. Settling in and making sure they understand what has happened to them. Settle any nerves or questions they might have.

Qn: Are there a lot of people that pass in the physical world that need to be directed towards the Light?
Chief: Yes. They may have things left undone, or a trauma caused by sudden and violent death....

Qn: And can death in war cause some of that?
Chief: Yes. When you die in, say, a hospital bed or in your sleep it can be peaceful, then you are looking for the next stage. However, if you have your energy ripped from your body, e.g. blown up, there is confusion, and you are left not always knowing what has happened or where you are, as the energy blast may have transported you across its path and you become disorientated and fearful.

Things are then seen as a threat, so you lock yourself away in a scenario you create for your own protection – this is an extreme example that I give – and then do not see us or any one until someone passes their way and breaks through their defences; this is when we can help them to find peace and love in the Light of the Creator.

Qn: What about someone who ignores the Light to stay in their home?
Chief: That is usually because they are focused on their possessions and their life and are reluctant to leave either. They do not realise that they can still go to the Light and return later to visit loved ones. This is important, by going into the Light it does not close you off from your family and loved ones, after you have settled you can hop back and forth between the Veil.

I wish to propose another thought. If life as you know it were to suddenly end, you may also find that leaving your body was a jolt or shock. If you have no knowledge and only fear of death, how do you break through to this individual. I ask this question as it has a pertinent answer, and it is one you are quite capable of finding the answer amongst our teachings.

Qn: *How do earthbound spirits sustain their energy?*
Chief: By using the area and its objects, even pets or people, etc. to draw from.

Qn: *When an individual dies, what happens to the Guides of an individual who does not pass to the Light?*
Conglomerate: You wish to inquire as to what happens to the spirit Guides while this individual is stuck in their situation. Do they wait around for this individual? The answer is no. It would be a complete waste of resources for them; they cannot get through to this individual because this person is not looking at or willing to acknowledge the Light, and the Light is where the Guides will be.

Qn: *So, an individual could be lost or remain earthbound for hundreds of years.*
Conglomerate: Or longer, because what has happened is that their vision and intention has been centred on what will be if they pass now and stay on the physical Level. Perhaps they have unfinished business and feel intentionally that there is something to finish and cannot do it. They miss the people that were standing beside them because they are intent on looking at the physical.

Now when you pass, you should all be looking for the Light, you will be looking for your friends or family. You will be looking around, but if something happens, or you are scared and you are looking down into the physical you will not see the higher Levels.

༄

Most earthbound spirits visiting the Circle were anxious to cross over into the Light once they had become aware of it, many not staying long enough to discuss their earthbound experiences. However, some expressed gratitude and stayed for a little while to briefly share some of their memories before being guided by other spirits to cross over into the Light.

Margaret[82]

Qn: ... Did you used to know me? (Yes). You were a friend of mine?
Margaret: Yes, in a way. I had the house a long time ago.

Qn: Was that before or after the incident.
Margaret: Before it was flattened by a Nazi bomb. Unfortunately, I took to under the stairs when the bombs dropped. The end was quick.

Qn: Did you hang around the house for quite a while afterwards? (Yes). Were you the lady that I kept glimpsing? (Yes). Then one day you just went, didn't you? (Yes). Why?
Margaret: Because I was content to leave my home with you.

Qn: Was that when you went into the Light? (Yes). You didn't like the people before us. (No). The door frame that you were trying to show me, was that where you were taking cover under the stairs. (Yes). Can you remember the address?
Margaret: You are most welcome. 32 Balliol Road.

---

82 Margaret had been the first owner of a house that we had bought and moved into in 1980. She had lived there since it had been built in the 1930s. The house had been bombed around 1942, wherein she had been killed whilst sheltering under the stairs during a bombing raid; the house was rebuilt in 1948. During the early years of our residence there, on several occasions our daughter (who is also now a Medium) had looked past me before settling down to sleep after saying 'goodnight nana' even though there was no one else in the room.

Qn: Yes, you're right it was, Margaret. Why are you here now?
Margaret: Book. You need some experience to add at the end of your writing.

Qn: How did you find us?
Margaret: Easy. The word is out there now, and they let come who they believe you would be able to use

Qn: Who contacted you?
Margaret: This was on the equivalent to a Notice Board[83]. By the way, I discovered later the bombs were the Nazi pilots discharging their pay load as they headed back, toots sweet[84].

Qn: When you leave here, where will you go to? (Home). *Where's home?*
Margaret: In a different dimension and vibration.

Qn: Are you aware of the different Levels and vibrations? (Yes). Do you travel down through the vibrations? (Yes). Do you travel up through the vibrations? (A little). Is your vibration level in the lower half of a Level? (Yes).

Qn: What are you seeing in this room right now?
Margaret: The room is dark but far from black, there are colours that emanate from you all.

Qn: Did you come here on your own? (No). Are there many with you?

---

83   It was later explained by a spirit Guide that Margaret was referring to a form of notice board in the spirit world advertising this book was being written and volunteers were needed to speak of their experiences!

84   English pronunciation of the French phrase 'tout de suite' which means very quickly or immediately. This became a common phrase around London in the 1940s.

Margaret: There are people all around.

Qn: Are these the people that came with you?
Margaret: Your Guides.

Qn: Have you got anything else to say?
Margaret: Goodbye, my friends.

Sally

Qn: Who are we talking with now? (Sally...) ... Have you been brought along to experience talking to us?
Sally: I had passed over 300 years ago. The journey to the Light was not easy for me, I was scared at first and turned away from the door of light that I saw. It was a time of trouble for me. I was not well educated and did not understand what I had been through. I hung in limbo for what must have been years; then I got assistance from someone who was passing. She held my attention and when the Light came, she walked happily into it and had people greet her. I followed her into the Light as it was closing. I then found I was no longer afraid.

Qn: Can you remember what you saw when you had passed over?
Sally: Lights and people.

Qn: Did you recognise those people around you in the Light? (No). *Did that frighten you?*
Sally: No. I am not sure why. I waited and others came to help me.

Qn: At what point did you recognise your family?
Sally: I did not know my family.

Qn: When you went to the Light did you see your family?
Sally: I had no family.

Qn: Sorry. Have you been in the Light a long time now?
Sally: Yes. I have a large group of family[85] and friends.

Qn: Are you in a community now? (Yes). How many met you when you passed over?
Sally: Three. I have passed over unannounced.

Qn: Did you know who the three were that met you?
Sally: Angels. They looked after me.

Qn: Do you live on your own? (No). Where do you live now?
Sally: In a street with others.

Qn: And does your street have other streets adjoining it? (Yes). What do you like to do? (Sing). Will you return to the physical world again soon?
Sally: No, much better here. It's free from fear, free from hunger. Full of life and laughter in the Light.

Charlie?[86]

Qn: Would you like to introduce yourself, please? (drew X)... Will you tell me where you come from. (drew X). Does this indicate you are not good at writing? (Yes). Can one of the Guide members help

---

85 Although Sally had previously said she had no family, she did have a spiritual family. I have noticed that some spirits returning to the Light refer to spirit friends as family even though they may not have been family in the physical world. It seems in spirit you have a wider spirit family.

86 I had no way of knowing whether Charlie was his proper name, and despite his illiteracy, he seemed to be the spokesperson for a group that wanted to cross into the Light. It seems that some may have been earthbound for possibly 500 years. Historical records showed that there may have been a mass grave near a churchyard in this vicinity of St Martins Church, Nibley North where battles had been fought nearby. It is recorded that skeletons were found when a wall by the church was being repaired a few years ago.

him to write please. Can you give us your name? (Charlie). Did you work at Berkeley Castle? (No). Did you used to live at Berkeley Castle? (No). Did you fight around Berkeley Castle? (Yes). Are you a Loyalist? (No response). Are you a Cromwellian Round Head?
Charlie: Catholic. Catholic.

Qn: Were you at Berkeley Castle during the period of the English Reformation? (Yes). Were you in the army? (No). Were you a pauper? (No). Can you tell me where you lived there?
Visitor: In the Castle.

Qn: Were you a servant?
Charlie: No, I was family of the owner. My name is Charlie.

Qn: Can you tell us about your life in the castle, please.
Charlie: It was fine. We had food and drink and warmth to keep out the cold. There was much trouble in the land, there was all the time. The castle was thrown into much turmoil, and I can tell you it changed, and so many times. There was much bloodshed in differing causes, that I saw much destruction. In my heart and my passing, I have witnessed stability, and this makes me happy to go now that all is well at last.

There are others you collected from a church from the mass grave. It is bewildering for them; they have little or no grasp of what has happened or why they have come. They just feel it was right to come. So, I ask you to help us all, regardless of creed or nation. We are all the same under his skies.

Qn: You are Catholic? (Yes). Are there many Catholics with you? (Yes). Others are Protestants? (Yes, and Welsh). Are all of you that came here from the castle here now. (Yes).

Two Spirits from Milan

Qn: ... I'm not very good at speaking Italian, can Gemma help translate for you[87].
Visitor: I lived in the theatre[88]; I worked at the costume management. I looked after and supervised the construction of costumes and kept them safe, hence I lived at the theatre.

Qn: Did you know Gemma? (No). Did you look after some clothing for Gemma? (Yes). Does Gemma know you? (Yes). How come you remained at the theatre for so long?
Visitor: Watching the costumes.

Qn: Why didn't you walk into the Light at the time of your passing?
Visitor: I could not leave the costumes. I did not look for the Light. I now know I should let go of this; I am ready now to enter the Light.

Qn: ... will the new visitor please introduce yourself.
Geraldo: I saw you in the square and you shone like a beautiful object[89], and I have followed that object so I can go now with the others into the Light. I am Geraldo. The only jobs I can do...

Qn: Geraldo what did you used to do?
Geraldo: I was a latrine officer or boy officer.

---

87 Sometimes a visiting spirit might speak in the language of their past life. Our Guide teams are multi-cultural, and Gemma is a Guide who lived in Italy in her last past life and had performed at La Scala as an opera singer. She works with one of the Mediums.

88 Teatro Alla Scala, Milan – A prestigious theatre renowned for its extensive costume collection and rich historical significance.

89 Another reference to the spiritual light emanating from the energy of individual in the physical. We cannot see the brightness of the Light on physical level. The brightness of spirit energy is dependent upon the spiritual Level of the individual it originally emanates from.

Qn: Well, does that mean you're in charge of bathing and cleanliness and toilet. (Yes). Where was that? (No response). Is this in Milano? (Castello)[90]. When?
Geraldo: Don't know.

Qn: I read that Leonardo da Vinci worked there in the 16th century for about 16 years.
Geraldo: Seventeen years, five months, 3 days[91].

Slouti[92]

Qn: ... Are you someone who wants to talk to us? (Yes). ... If you cannot write in a language that we would understand, please pass your words to one of the spirit Guides here and they will write for you or with you.
Visitor: I write. SLOUTI. (The name had to be written and re-written several times as none of those present could understand the name given or the language, the conversation was carried out with difficulty. I remain unsure whether this name is the correct one.)

Qn: Are you a gentleman? Are you a lady? Are you a young man? Are you a child? We are trying to establish whether you're a lady or a man. Are you a male? Are you a female? (No responses). Please come back and talk to us. Don't be insulted that I could not pronounce

---

90 Geraldo was probably referring to Sforzesco Castle in Milan.

91 No idea where that came from or why and have no means of checking either!

92 At first, we had difficulty establishing who the spirit was and where he had come from. We persevered and I can only conclude from the conversation and historical research that Slouti is an Egyptian servant from possibly the 19th Dynasty (1292 BC to 1189 BC) who had devotedly served his Master through life and death.

your name or understand you. I have spelt it out several times and also have this on the recording. So please, where has this person come from? Are you happy now? (Yes). Let's start again. Are you an adult male? (Yes). Did you come back with us from a place we recently visited?
Slouti: Kingston Lacey.

Qn: Did you work there. (No). Did you live there?
Slouti: I was in spiritual residence.

Qn: ... Did you accompany one of the art items that had been collected from around the world? (Yes). Was one of those items something that belonged to you? (Yes). Was it a painting? (No). Did you live in the Priory at Lacy? (No). But you just said you were in spiritual residence. (Yes). And the Priory is the spiritual building.
Slouti: I am older than the Priory and House, I learnt.

Qn: Have you been there since before the Priory was built?
Slouti: No. I came with my stone.

Qn: Stone? Can you tell me what you've been doing all this time?
Slouti: I have guarded my tablet; it should not have been removed from my Masters tomb. I was in charge of looking after him in this world and the next.[93]

Qn: So, you were there before the Priory and House was built?
Slouti: No. I came with the stone tablet.

---

93   In accordance with belief of that time, Slouti may well have been still alive when placed in the tomb of his Master. The tablet referred to may be one of a number that came into the possession of William Bankes in the early 19th century and held at Kingston Lacy ever since (they are worth seeing).

Qn: Are you Egyptian? (Yes). And what made you decide to follow us?
Slouti: You sensed me, and I sensed you. Your Guides made me aware of the situation. I watch others cross. Now I understand it is my turn.

Qn: Could you please describe what you have been doing in the physical world since you died?
Slouti: Watching over my sun and life since we passed into his tomb. I have died doing this and continued to do so. I followed the people that stole from my Master. I now understand that my beliefs may not be the ones held now, and I wish to join my Master in the afterlife. I can pay my way, and I see the boat before me. I will now take it and cross into the afterlife. Thank you for all your help.

Qn: … How did that just happen?
Chief: We help him. We needed no distraction. We all needed to be calm and focused on the job at hand.

Qn: He seems to have been a guardian of a stone tablet for a very, very long time.
Chief: More than 2000 years.

Qn: What state is he in? Could you explain?
Chief: He is fine. He sat in a place where visitors come, and he topped himself up. A man who does not understand the modern way. You will not feel so tired now. A man who was used to taking what he needed or wanted in the name of his Master.

Qn: Does that mean that he was pulling on our energy a bit? (Yes).

Qn: …. Has anything interesting happened to you recently, CP?
CP: Yes. Met a funny guy so different from us, his belief system does not commute to ours. I am wondering how many there are across the

Universe. Guess what. There was a black dog headed man sailing the boat that collected him.

Qn: Can you tell me what that means? Was this associated with his belief? (Yes). Ah, if you have to pay the ferryman so to speak...
CP: Dog man.[94]

Qn: Could he see for all that time?
CP: Yes. Not a lot, his focus was on his Masters coffin for a long time. Time does not go in the same way, and it is easy to get lost in it.

Qn: Suspended animation ......
CP: No. Stasis.

ಞ

I considered for some time whether it would be appropriate to publish the conversations with earthbound spirits and concluded that sharing this information is essential for understanding the events that may transpire when an individual is transitioning back to the spirit realm. I think the conversations with these earthbound spirits have yielded valuable insights and enhanced our growing understanding of the spirit world, while also presenting some evidence as to why some spirits missed or disregarded the opportunity to enter the Light. Interestingly, it was evident from those spirits that did speak with the Circle, their experiences were very focused and limited.

In certain rare instances, an earthbound spirit may exhibit disruptive behaviour and display an unwillingness to return to

---

94 The reference by CP to a man with the head of a black dog steering a boat likely pertains to Anubis. In ancient Egyptian belief, Anubis, often depicted as a human adorned in gold with the head of a black dog, was thought to ferry spirits across a river to the afterlife (Duat). Perhaps this is also demonstrating just how spirit can use the energy to re-enact or re-create the expectations and belief of an individual to help ease their way back to the Light and/or their heaven..

the Light. This hesitation can be attributed to their disbelief in or a lack of understanding regarding the significance of the Light. It is also possible that such spirits simply wished to continue their solitary existence completely unaware that they have become bothersome to individuals in the physical world. So, what measures can be taken when a troublesome earthbound spirit is eventually located but still refuses to cross over into the Light?

Qn: When a troublesome spirit is located but still does not wish to go to the Light, how do you deal with them?
Chief: It depends. If they are interfering with another existence in a bad way, then we can remove them by utilising some skills which we can bring into force that can lock or restrain the aforesaid rogue spirit and he or she will be brought before the tribunal that will decide what is best for them. Whether this is help with education or rebirth or, if it is more complex, then several other methods will be brought into play. We will do our utmost to accommodate the best for the individual spirit, but some behaviour cannot be expunged, and you take that karma as a burden that it will continue to grow unless it is expunged and you develop a clean slate, then all the choices are yours to make.

Qn: Are there any circumstances when a spirit is allowed to remain on the physical Level?
Chief: Yes. Your Guides are an example.

Qn: If spirit Guides are no longer present after the individual has passed and is alone, will the individual still be allowed to remain on the physical Level?
Chief: They will remain until they choose to cross to the Light.

Qn: If the individual had been an atheist throughout their life what happens when they die?
Chief: They get a bit of a surprise. Remember, it is not religiously driven and my idea of what would happen is different from many others. But ultimately it is the same for all.

As part of Rita's journey as a spiritual Medium, she has been called upon to interact with earthbound spirits, often under challenging or distressing circumstances, to help her spirit Guides persuade an earthbound spirit that has been located to cross into the Light. She is not unique in this endeavour; there are other spiritual Mediums in the physical world who follow similar paths. But this role necessitates having a strong link and collaboration with her spirit Guides. In such a situation where a troublesome earthbound spirit cannot be persuaded to cross over, other high-level spirits may be summoned to ensure the earthbound spirit's enforced return to the Light.

Higher Conscious

After all that you have read thus far, do you now think that your core may be a spirit energy with an infinite existence? Maybe you are still not convinced because you have no recollection of the infinite existence that you are supposed to have had and need explanations for why you can only remember experiences and events from your current physical existence. I agree that it is perfectly reasonable to anticipate having memories of other past lives that you may have experienced in the physical realm, along with recollections of an infinite existence in the spirit realm. If that were the case, it would provide undeniable evidence of an infinite afterlife. The doubts and scepticisms that individuals may hold in this area are entirely understandable.

Some attendees at Circle sittings have expressed similar concerns, which I also shared during the very early days communicating with spirits. However. Spirits always maintained that memories of life in the spirit world or past physical lives could not be accessed for various reasons and these memories are stored separately in what they describe as our higher consciousness, preserved until they can be accessed again when each individual returns to the spirit world.

In the following discussions, spirits have provided some notable insights regarding the fate of our personal memories as an individual's spirit energy transitions between the spiritual and physical worlds. Terms such as 'higher collective,' 'higher consciousness,' 'higher self,' and 'higher conscious' refer to the same concept; an area beyond our direct access that stores memories from the various lives and existences that has been experienced by each individual spirit. Naturally, the number of incarnations or existences achieved will depend on the age of the spirit energy rather than the physical age of the individual. Consequently, older spirits are likely to have undergone more experiences compared to a young spirit energy.

Qn: Can you tell us where the memories of our past lives in spirit are held?
Lady: Yes. It is part of the collective, part of the higher collective.

Qn: What do you mean by part of the higher collective?
Lady: It is part of your stored memories and information that you can access at any time when you are in spirit.

Qn: Can we access it physically?
Lady: Yes. Some may bridge the divide, and some may experience a leakage.

Qn: If some people bridge the divide, can they access all their stored information? (No). *Is all our information and memories stored for us?* (Yes). *Is the higher self with us all the time, within our aura?*
Lady: No, it is not situated within. Not within you.

Qn: Could you elaborate on whether the higher self is within a person's aura field.
Lady: It is not in your aura field.

Qn: Can it be accessed from within our aura field?
Lady: Yes, you can, but it is not stored within your aura field.

Qn: Then is it held above us?
Lady: In the collective.

Qn: What is the collective?
Lady: The collective is energy.

Qn: Is this energy in a single place? Just one collective of energy where it is all stored?
Lady: No, there are many access points.

Qn: Does that mean we have our memories cleared and stored for us before we enter a new physical life? (Yes). Do we get it all back? (Yes). You say that there is a higher self that stores our memories whilst we come down to a physical life on Earth, and this memory will be retrieved when we return to spirit and covers everything that we have ever done, and that living this physical life is only temporary and so memories were taken away for that purpose. Is this right? (Yes). Thank you, would you share just a little bit more knowledge with us? (Yes). What Level are you from?
Lady: Masters and Prophets.[95]

ಌ

The discussion was continued later with the Conglomerate, where more detailed answers were provided.

Qn: My sub-conscious is stored somewhere for me, why can't I access it?
Conglomerate: Yes, it is, but let's look at it this way. You have between here and there a block. The block will not allow or rather is not supposed to allow the memories of past lives to drip through; this ensures that you can start your new life experience with as clear a beginning as possible. If you brought all your past life memories

---

95   Level 2.

with you, you would not enjoy your current physical existence here, because the lessons and things that had happened to you in the past would make you so nervous about what could happen now that you would not be able to settle, you would not enjoy. For example, I believe your friend has already inquired about this, that their past life was not satisfactorily ended[96] as one would have wished to have had it ended. This means that you would still bear all the memories of the pain and of the circumstances in which your demise took place. Now, how do you think that would impact upon your next life experience?

Qn: Is this block also the Veil that you have previously told us about?
Conglomerate: This is the barrier between your knowledge that you hold in your energy and the knowledge that you can ascertain in your energy[97]. There are very few people where the barrier might break down and which could result in them getting problems and issues from multiple personalities that might come through because of this being who they were in the past. So, you must understand that the barrier is there for your own good.

If you could imagine that there is your energy and the physical brain that you have now. The recollections you have are from the physical brain where you have learnt things by experience. You have your spiritual brain with you that knows things and enables you to see things until you grow older; maybe then you don't see those things anymore because your physical brain has taken over. There are those that remain more connected to their energy, which

---

96 The Circle member to whom the Conglomerate was addressing the answer had previously received answers to questions about a past life in the physical which had not ended well.

97 The Conglomerate is referring to the knowledge that we learn during our current physical life, and that knowledge which is held for us in the energy as part of our earlier existences, both of which are ultimately separated by the block.

means they are more connected to their spiritual side.

If you can imagine a tube running to another part of your brain, because you all understand brains, don't you? So, if you imagine your energy as having a part here and a part there, and there is a tube that connects these two parts, and that tube, for the time being, has been cut. This means that part of your energy is stuck there, and the other part of your energy is living the physical existence with you here. Now, when you depart this physical existence and you go on into your proper spiritual existence, the block or cut is removed or repaired and the two parts rejoin and the energy flows together again, bringing with it all of what you have learnt in the past. The speed at which this will happen depends upon the speed at which you are capable of receiving those memories when in spirit.

For example, it could suddenly send you into complete uproar if immediately after your passing from your physical life, in comes all the knowledge. You will think you have gone insane, and it is too much for the mind to work out, even though you will now be in spirit. Of course, there are some that can gain all their knowledge very quickly because they understand what is happening, as they are closer to their spiritual self and they will either get it joined up by a little drip at a time, or it just goes zap when the tube is opened. Does that put it in a way that you can perhaps understand?

You must remember you are made of energy. When you go into spirit and pass through the Veil into the spiritual dimension, you are energy. Your physical body is energy. It is easy to separate energy and bring it back together, much easier than chopping your physical brain in half and bringing it back together. You see, within your energy you store a lot of information. Everything you have learned in your physical existence will be stored in your energy and you will take all that knowledge back with you into spirit. You will come to terms with everything that has happened in your physical life, and you will pass on any knowledge that you feel is worthy of being overtime and depending on how much you wish to access you may not want to know. You may decide you are quite happy with your current existence and wish to leave your old memories stored for a later date, that is perfectly feasible and acceptable, but you might upset one or two people who were in your past life. If you ignore them, I am sure they will understand.

Qn: Are the higher conscious and the subconscious the same thing?
Conglomerate: It is difficult to understand. We have called it the higher consciousness because it is energy. You have a subconscious within your physical brain and, when you don't use all your brain, we call it your subconsciousness.

When your body shuts and goes to sleep, your body goes into subconsciousness, but your spirit does not, your spirit is still active, still conscious, as it does not need to sleep. That is why we call it higher consciousness.

Qn: Do our spirits retain everything?
Conglomerate: Our spirit's higher consciousness is absorbing information through all your physical lives, as well as your everlasting spiritual existence.

Qn: Does the individual memory that I have belong to me?
Conglomerate: That is yours. It can be accessed by the Source but cannot be accessed by others unless you blend, or you give permission. The Source does not need permission.

Qn: I do not understand how in my physical life I cannot remember my higher consciousness.
Conglomerate: That is deliberate, for if you came down with all these memories you would not be able to exist to follow your path within this physical world.

Qn: So, my higher consciousness is there with me, but I cannot access it until I go back to the spirit world.
Conglomerate: Yes, and then only when you wish to. It is there for you should you require it. It does not always come back instantly, for there is a period of adjustment. When a desire to know comes, you may find that you have made the right adjustment a lot faster than the average person.

Qn: Where is information about our spirit existence stored?
Conglomerate: In your higher consciousness.

Qn: Is it possible for me to talk to my higher consciousness or to access it?
Conglomerate: It is possible to be shown parts of it. It would be a case of your spirit accessing it.

Qn: Is it possible for one of our spirit Guides to access the higher consciousness to enable an individual to talk to it? And for that Guide to tell that individual what has been said?
Conglomerate: I am thinking of this as a conundrum. If you mean talking to a person's higher self, then their ordinary physical self would need to be still, because otherwise your whole being would be involved in your body just sitting and being here. You would benefit from being in a hypnotic state; in fact, in that state your spirit is a bit freer.

Sometimes when you are in a hypnotic state, like in a game show where they tell you that you are a chicken, all you are affecting is the mind. You are on a superfluous level and some people are very susceptible to it as it affects the mind and tells the mind what it is. If you go deeper into hypnosis, so that your spirit is free to talk and see, then you may be allowed to access some of your memory.

It would depend a lot on what your Guardian[98] thought it would be wise for you to access, and of course for the purpose you are there, you may be there to bring knowledge through this medium. So, it is not as straightforward as one would like to say yes, it is not that straightforward. Also, you find that people who respond to hypnosis and go back into their past lives may already be quite spiritual, because their spirit is more able to allow others to communicate through them. Does that make sense to you?

Qn: Just looking for a straight answer that can be understood.
Conglomerate: You have done it already when you ask for healing. You are healing when you are asking somebody if they will receive healing, and you cannot physically ask them. You ask their higher self, and their higher self decides whether you can access the spiritual and physical body of the person concerned. So, the higher self can still operate, it is not dead and is still an active part of you. It is just not able to communicate efficiently between A and B.

Qn: I understand that it is not accessible, but if permission is given to one of our dedicated Guides, would they be able to access and talk to the higher self for us?
Conglomerate: It all depends. After some consultation[99], it depends. It depends how much it would interfere with the life path the person is on. You see, the questions you ask may divert ... there is an issue of concern... the reason memories are locked away is because it can interfere with your current physical life. If everybody starts talking to their higher self and is getting information, it is not always productive. The questions you ask may not be the right question,

---

[98] One of the main four spirit Guides who are with us throughout our physical life.

[99] There appeared to be a consultation held between other members of the Conglomerate before the response was completed.

but it may give you an answer that is not the right answer that you really need.

Qn: I was hoping to ask my higher conscious about my own life in spirit, not about past physical lives or how I am doing on my path.
Conglomerate: But your life in spirit will be totally different. You will take back all what you have experienced, learnt, sought out, done, all the rest, so when you go back you may think I am going to change what I did because I much prefer this era or that era. You might redesign everything so your life in the past in spirit was one way and when you go back to this time you might just change it.

The Conglomerate had put forward several compelling reasons for why a physical life will only start with just the basic instinct to survive to avoid what has been described as potential mental chaos! However, I did find some of the Conglomerate's latter responses intriguing, which prompted me to consider conducting an experiment by trying to communicate with my higher conscious. To do this I would need the agreement and cooperation of a spirit Guide to act as an intermediary. It was the Chief who agreed to act as the intermediary, who is identified in the conversation as Guide (HC). Physical energy was used for the demonstration and the responses were written on the table.

Qn: Am I now able to directly communicate with my higher consciousness? (No). Well, if I wanted to try this through a Guide or another spirit, would you be able to do this?
Guide (HC): Ask the question.

Qn: What am I when I am in spirit?

Guide (HC): Silly question, it is energy.

Qn: ... *what type of energy?*
Guide (HC): Spiritual energy.

Qn: *Are there different types of spiritual energy?*
Guide (HC): Different vibrations, different make up of memory. How do you think you blend easily?

Qn: *I don't know, that is why I'm asking these questions.*
Guide (HC): Then you will have to wait and see.

Qn: *What is my role and my life like in spirit?*
Guide (HC): Busy. Part time messenger.

Qn: *And what do I do?*
Guide (HC): Carry important information and knowledge to whoever it needs to be directed to.

Qn: *Who provides me with these messages?*
Guide (HC): Various sources, but not the Source.

Qn: *You say that I am part time, so when I'm not delivering messages what do I do the other time?*
Guide (HC): Enjoy your villa on a cliff top by the sea.

Qn: *Do I live in darkness?* (No). *What do I live in?* (Energy). *Is the energy blank?*
Guide (HC): No, it is energy. You are made up from energy and you can see in the sun's energy.

Qn: *What do I see around me when in spirit?*
Guide (HC): People who are around via your chosen place. Here in

this physical world, all life and you are still made up of energy, even the body you now inhabit is just energy. The molecules and atoms spin at a speed and vibration that enables this planet and world to exist in your eyes. Throw off the physical, which eventually goes to dust and feed, you can still exist and carry on as before except that you do not need to eat or to sleep because you are attached to the eternal energy supplier.

Qn: Have I ever travelled far? (Yes). Could you tell me where or how?
Guide (HC): Curiosity strikes us all. We are all guilty of looking to the stars and wondering what is out there in the beauty of creation.

Qn: What is my most important achievement in spirit?
Guide (HC): It depends on what you give each rating to events. For at the time, they are all momentous.

Qn: What has been my most important achievement as a messenger?
Guide (HC): Getting to be one.

Qn: Thank you for an interesting experiment. Just as a matter of interest, have I been talking directly to my higher consciousness? (No). Has somebody been interpreting? (Yes). And who has been interpreting for me?
Chief: Me, the Chief.

Qn: Thank you Chief. My higher consciousness said that I am a part-time messenger in spirit, taking and delivering messages. (Yes). How far might I have had to travel to deliver these messages?
Chief: All over the dimensions. You have a free pass, so to speak. You can adjust your vibration. You are good at what you do.

Qn: My higher consciousness also said that my spirit energy blends easily.

Chief: Yes, to deliver messages that are private[100].

Qn: If I 'enjoy time in a villa' when not messaging, do I also visit others? (Yes). Including time visiting friends of the Native American culture.
Chief: To visit CP and others.

Qn: Had I delivered messages to my physical partner when she was in spirit? (No). Then how did I get to know her?
Chief: You met a long time ago. You walked the Earth together.

※

So, it does now seem all the more plausible that memories from an individual's past lives are stored in a higher consciousness, awaiting access upon return to the spirit realm. However, a pertinent question remains: how straightforward is it to recover those memories, and what process must an individual undergo to achieve this?

Qn: We come down multiple times, how does the memory come back when an individual returns to spirit and can we access all those lives we may have lived?
Conglomerate: Firstly, you will pass over in the last presence, the last life and you need to learn to adjust into the spirit world again. Then it comes like a book that you can delve into and out of so you can adjust fully and with lots of time and love. Some lives are best only to remember the life lesson and that value, the rest may be undesirable and therefore you find that it is best left in that chapter, closed. I feel that it is best to slowly absorb the information, or you would go

---

100 The blending between spirits also appears to be used for the purpose of private conversation.

insane. It would be difficult to disseminate between reality now and those past life experiences. So great care is taken, all lives, no matter how small, are recorded, for it beholds us to keep this treasure of your life experiences in life's special record.

Qn: Is it possible for spirits to visit the Circle to discuss what happened to them as they got their memories back.
Chief: You know the answer already. It cannot be quantified as all of us experience it differently. No two are the same. So many choices. So many different times. So, it is impossible to generate a one for all role on memory regaining. Also, the length of time for the spirit to readjust.

Celia

Qn: I was just hoping to be able to use an example in the book that might reflect a spirit's feelings as their memories come back. I appreciate the scope is endless. For example, are memories reabsorbed?
Visitor: Yes. I am Celia.

Qn: Can you tell us how you reabsorbed your memory when you passed. (No response). Did you pass a long time ago? (No). So, you have recently passed. (Yes). At some point you recovered your greater memories.
Celia: Not a lot at once. Just a prompting of my lives in a book of me. This allowed a drip feeding of some information.

Qn: Were you able to separate that part which was your physical lives and those of your existence in spirit?
Celia: Not at first. It was confusing. There was so much to understand and to come to grips and terms with. I understand that I have had many lives before, and I am only glimpsing some of the associated memories when I go into a meditative state to allow my consciousness

to expand and regress into my past and I learned more of myself.

Qn: As you reabsorb more knowledge about yourself, are you able to categorise each memory into each life that you had?
Celia: I have a small number in each and some lives. I have not explored them all yet. But when I come out of that state, I have an understanding and more knowledge. I suppose it is like going to school. I am learning slowly.

Qn: You said you wanted to explore and you're going to explore more of your lives. How do you do it? Does it come in as memory. Or do you see it visually?
Celia: Meditation opens the mind to expand to reveal all. Like when you remember in physical.

Qn: You are telling us is that it's a slow learning or reabsorption process? (Yes). Once you have accessed all your memories, will all of it stay with you?
Celia: Yes. You can compartmentalise the stuff that is unimportant.

Judith

Qn: Judith, welcome. Are you here to chat with us? (Yes). Have you recently passed? (No). Have you come from the Light? (Yes). Have you come here to chat with us? (Yes). Can you tell us what you remember about getting your first glimpse of a past life memory?
Judith: Yes. It was in a book in the hall of records. It gave details of my life in the physical I had just left. It was very accurate, good and bad. I then looked at another volume, it was of me in another physical life. I read a little but did not recognise myself then. So, I was advised to expand my mind in a quiet place, and snippets returned. It is I suppose like creating a link to my past and this is available should I wish to access it. There were many volumes so I do not know what

I will find out in my search. I may not wish to follow all up over a short while, as I am not sure I want all the bad bits back.

Qn: So, all your physical lives are stored as individual volumes. (Yes). You can access these anytime you want to. (Yes). You don't have to access them, but they are there for you if you wish, and it may not be a good thing to carry them around with you. (Yes). Is your existence in the spirit world also in held in volumes or is it now part of your memory? (Memory). So, in spirit, physical lives are tucked away. (Yes). But your spiritual memory is with you all the time, because that is you. (Yes). When you went back into the spirit world after your last physical life, did your spiritual memory come back to you quickly? (Slower). Are your memories of spirit good memories? (Yes). To help explain a bit more, can you tell us about some of your good memories?

Judith: The people that are my close friends. The learning I have established. That all comes back as the fog of confusion dissipates.

Qn: When you entered the Light, had you still retained your physical memory? (Yes). Was it progressively replaced by your spiritual memory?

Judith: No. You still hold the memory of your last physical existence close to hand.

Qn: So, when you return to the Light you are still carrying the memories of your previous life in the physical with you because that is who you are? (Yes). Then your spiritual memory gradually comes back. Is that what happens? (Emerges). Emerges. Your spiritual memories start to emerge? (Yes). Thank you, Judith. Did you get a surprise when you passed to spirit? (Yes).

Olive

Qn: Are you part of my friendship family? (Yes). When we get together, what do we do?
Olive: Sometimes when events allow, we meet socially.

Qn: What do we do socially?
Olive: Same as you do in the physical mostly. Talk, say what we have been up to. Some are delicate and private for an individual, so we must always remember our Charges. It would not do, for example to say they chinked it. It would not be acceptable to gossip about it. It has happened a lot in past years. But you can talk about their graduation and positive achievements.

Qn: Do we keep up to date with what's happened in all our group's lives?
Olive: Yes. My mother was always updating everyone on my life, only she was a little embarrassing and I felt I had to remind her many times.

Qn: All mothers are alike, they're very proud of their children. (Yes). How will a returning spirit be able to recognise someone from their friendship group in spirit without their memories in spirit?
Olive: Given time. Not a case of me telling them.

Qn: Do those memories return?
Olive: Yes. That is spiritual knowledge. The rest are chapters in your development to be read, and the lessons taken, then shelved away for future reference if you so require it.

Qn: Regaining memory is not a single light bulb moment then?
Olive: No. That would create a dual personality split.

Sounds incredible, but it seems there are extensive energy libraries that hold records of each of our physical lives. I hope that you have found the explanations given by spirits quite plausible, but I leave you to draw your own conclusions from the discussions. It does seem that when returning to spirit there are many choices for the individual to make about how they intend to resume their infinite spiritual existence with whom and however, and I totally get it why returning spirits may take a while to recognise themselves when they may read or learn about other past physical lives they may have had, both good and bad.

Visitors from the Past

Many visiting spirits were previously unknown to participants attending the Circle. Most likely, these visits served as a means for spirits to be acknowledged and demonstrate their continuing existence in the afterlife. Some of the interactions provided Circle attendees with opportunities to engage in meaningful and interesting dialogue with spirits from diverse backgrounds, including contemporary celebrities and historical figures. Despite the unfamiliarity with visiting spirits most interactions were brief and pleasant.

Here are extracts from the discussions conducted with well-known individuals from the past. Following the discussions, I researched any notable information provided to try to verify the accuracy of their accounts after their visit. The four lines of poetry by WW amused the four Circle participants attending that evening, the footnotes are drawn up from research on the internet.

William Wordsworth

Qn: What is your name?
Visitor: William Wordsworth.

Qn: William Wordsworth. Good gracious me. Tell us about yourself please.
William: I am a writer and poet. I am a writer of all things. I look and I see a host....

Qn: of dancing daffodils. Yes, we know it well.
William: Golden daffodils. Golden[101].

Qn: How did you get into writing?
William: I found that words tripped off my tongue to please those that come on my very language. I found later I could also make a pretty... *(stopped suddenly)* ... How do you say, I am back. I had failed to pen my last sentence to perfection. I am not an uneducated man, I felt I could express life better if I said it in poem. Like: –

> "I see before me on a cloud of grey,
> three sights of beauty and a boy of grey,
> I feel their love for thirst of knowledge,
> and join within their Circle of love."

Qn: Have you just said a poem about this Circle tonight? (Yes).

Qn: Which is your favourite poem written?
William: Beloved[102], dear Lady.

Qn: What areas of Britain inspired you to write those beautiful poems?
William: The Downs. I have travelled far, and feel the Downs and counties are my favourites, apart from one special area north of the country

---

101 Historical records show that WW changed the description of the daffodils from "dancing" used in the original poem he penned in 1804, to the more familiar "golden" daffodils when he revised the poem in 1815.

102 I searched the internet but could not find a poem that WW might have written titled Beloved, unless he is referring to an unpublished work of his. However, I did discover the name of a book titled *Beloved* and published in 2019 which is a compilation of the poems that had been written by his sister, Dorothy. I can only surmise that this may have been WW's way of proving awareness of on-going physical events relating to their poetry. Had I known at the time of the sitting I would have asked. WW has not made a return visit.

Qn: What was your favourite possession?
William: A pen and paper.

Qn: Which school or college inspired you the most?
William: I was inspired more by writers like the great Bard, an uneducated man who wrote from his heart, his sonnets are a benchmark for all writers.

Qn: What do you do in spirit now?
William: Visit other writers, those that can listen, and help them in their life's work.

Qn: Have you visited the spiritual library? (Yes). How would you describe it.
William: Huge. Lots of books.

Qn: Can you describe its exterior?
William: A building like a Tardis[103], of course across dimensions.

Robert Clive

Qn: Can you tell us your name? (Robert). Robert, where did you join us from?
Robert: My home.

Qn: Where is your home?
Robert: Powis Castle.

---

103   An odd description to use given that Tardis is drawn from the 1960s. Perhaps like footnote 102, what is learned or heard in the physical world can also become known and quoted back from the spirit world!

Qn: Have you been to the Light?
Robert: Yes. I like my home, so I visit it often. We still gather there from time to time. Pleasure is a wonderful thing, and it gives us great pleasure to drop in from time to time and visit the old place.

Qn: What business were you involved with?
Robert: It was where money originated from. Trade and inheritance.

Qn: Immense wealth? (Yes). What did you learn from having all that wealth?
Robert: You don't need it when you pass through the Veil. You cannot take it with you in that sense.

Qn: Has it made you a better spiritual person.
Robert: You learn from your existence here in your own dimension, but you are a combination of all your learning when you join us.

Qn: What is your surname? (Clive).

Qn: Ah. Robert Clive. Please tell me briefly about your life.
Robert: Not so rich at start, but as a young man I was seeking a fortune in the continent of Asian India, and I had links with the East India Company and English Government. It was profitable for them to have power in the right hands, and this often required our services to remove certain people and put others in charge of work areas and culturally people, to keep the control in the East India Company. This was not pleasant but worked, but extraordinarily well rewarded on both sides of the coin. I became wealthy beyond belief. But this era was short lived, and what does one do when one has offended so many lives.

Qn: Were you invited to go over to North America. (Yes). Did you turn it down?

Robert: Yes. No wealth there.

Qn: Wealth was your driver? (Yes). Do you regret that now?
Robert: Yes, to some extent. I do not regret the money I passed on to my family or the good it has done, or how I got or obtained it, or for favours that I did.

Qn: You said that you still gather as a family at Powis Castle, even though you didn't own it.
Robert: Yes. Party time. My family did own it.

Qn: What was your most treasured possession?
Robert: My pipe.

Qn: Is it true you smoked heroin or poppy?
Robert: Yes, to drown the memories and feel good.

Qn: Are you happy now?
Robert: Yes. The knife, though requested by me, was not administered by me. It was an Indian manservant that administered it for me.

Qn: I do appreciate you coming to talk to us and being honest like this.
Robert: Thank you for listening to my words. It allowed me to get things off my chest.[104]

---

[104] This is what I researched after the visit.
Robert Clive (1725-1774) lived his early life in Shropshire, 40 miles from Powis Castle. His father was a parliamentarian and lawyer of modest income who secured employment for his son with the East India Company at the age of 19 years. Robert rose to the rank of Major General and became known as 'Clive of India'. He had a fearless reputation, which clearly helped him to secure much of India for Britain over the French. It has also been said that he may have used opium at times to combat gallstones and bouts of depression. Clive became a very wealthy individual from his business interests with Trade and Supply contracts and hand

Gyantwachia (Cornplanter)

CP first identified himself many years ago as a half-brother from a previous physical life. Although we use the familiar name of CP, he is often recognised by his American first nation birth name, Gyantwachia. He has been a significant spiritual presence at numerous Circle sittings, helping the Chief manage the physical energy and ensuring a safe conclusion to each sitting. There have been many times when he has had the Circle in stitches with his playful antics with the drum and humorous comments.

Qn: CP were you with me since birth? (No). Are you here to help with the physical energy work? (Yes). Please tell us about yourself in spirit.
CP: I am handsome. Well built. Romantic. Good in stature and have a large family.[105]

overs from the Indian rulers as rewards for helping to depose their enemies. The Asian Indian museum at Powis Castle was opened in his name to show the many exhibits from India that he had acquired in his lifetime and is well worth a visit.

Clive's wealth clearly brought on jealousy and suspicions about his activities in India, and he faced accusations of causing the Indian famine from which millions may have died but was eventually cleared by Parliament of any malpractice. He died at the age of 49 years and is said to have committed suicide at his Berkeley Square, London, home by slitting his jugular vein with a small blunt pen knife he had placed on his desk.

Robert Clive's association with Powis Castle seems to be through his son, Edward, who married the daughter of the previous Castle owner. Some of Robert Clive's wealth was used to pay off Edward's father-in-law's considerable debts.

105 CP's vain description of himself did caused amusement to those present but an article by Ed Byers (Pennsylvania WILDS) dated 28 April 2022 on Gyantwachia's life throughout the 18th century does seem to bear out a similar description through his parental lineage,

Qn: You forgot that good humour of yours, but in your natural spirit form, how do you look?
CP: The same.

Qn: The Chief has described his natural form as an orb. Are you similar?
CP: No, I am myself. I describe my last physical existence.

Qn: Can you describe your spirit identity.
CP: I am your accompaniment; I work and walk with you.

*Qn: What does your spirit look like? (*Energy*). What does your energy look like?*
CP: Whatever I want

*Qn: What colour is your Energy? (*Light*).*

Qn: Tell us something about yourself.
CP: That tells you a lot I was also good with the tongue and was a Diplomat.

Qn: Tell us what your hobbies were and what was your favourite colour?
CP: It was blue and green. Blue of the sky when it is kind to the people and nature below it. And green for the abundance that nature produces for one and for all. Not just humans you understand.

Qn: What food did you enjoy most?
CP: After the hunt, a big feast.

Qn: What was your favourite animal.
CP: Deer. They run and jump like the wind.

Qn: What did you live in. (Hut). *That be of wood?*
CP: We had plenty. We also had had a form of mobile shelter made from animal skin.

Qn: Did you use the mobile shelter for when you went hunting? (Yes). *Were there a lot of Buffalo?*
CP: Not so many, more moose and that family, and bear. We were in the northern section.

Qn: Were there some buffalo? (Yes). *When you went hunting, did you go individually?* (No). *Did you go as a group?* (Yes). *What did you use when hunting?*
CP: Arrows, spears, and much later guns.

Qn: What did you enjoy most in your last physical life.
CP: Silly question.

Qn: LOL. What was your most memorable achievement?
CP: I think it was my family, then Washington.

Qn: Can you tell us briefly about Washington.
CP: I was awarded a token of gratitude and peace. Not that it lasted, as you well know. They massacred us by attrition.

Qn: What was your happiest moment? (Peace). *And what was your saddest moment?* (War). *What was that token?* (Tomahawk). *Do you still carry it about?*
CP: I have my copy.

Qn: You've created it out of energy. (Yes). *Do you have any free time when you are not looking after your Charge?* (No). *So, what are you doing most of the time?*
CP: I watch, help, walk alongside.

Qn: Are you enjoying the job that you are doing?
CP: Yes. It is my job.

Qn: What is one of the most memorable things that you have accomplished in spirit?
CP: Becoming a Guide to others, and to help you.

Qn: Thank you CP. With this work you are doing, are you progressing? (Yes). Can you describe how you are progressing?
CP: When I go back, if I have achieved a favourable outcome, I will raise my vibration.

Johnny Cash

Qn: Who are you? (Johnny). Do you know anyone here? (No). Are you a boy? (No). Why have you come to see us this evening?
Johnny: Entertainment, singer, songwriter, musician.

Qn: Where did you play? (Prison). What was the name of the prison?
Johnny: The big one, starts with S[106].

Qn: Did your music get into the top 10? (Yes). What is your surname?
Johnny: Begin with C. No money. I am less.

Qn: Is this Johnny Cash?
Johnny: You tell me.

Qn: Where were you born?
Johnny: In Kingsland.

---

106 Johnny Cash is mostly associated with Folsom Prison due to recording an album of his live performance there, but he also played at the San Quentin state prison, the largest in California.

Qn: Was there one song you liked singing the most?
Johnny: A boy named Sue. It is always a laugh.

Qn: Anything you regret?
Johnny: Yes, being a bad boy at times and serving a bit of time in local jails on several occasions myself.

Qn: You liked drinking?
Johnny: Pretty ladies.

Qn: Were you always one for the ladies.
Johnny: Yes. It could have been three times.[107]

Qn: Who was your favourite singer?
Johnny: Elvis had a bit of a voice. Chuck Berry was also one I admired; he had a bit of a past like me.

Qn: Are you liking being in spirit?
Johnny: Yes. Get to see lots of pretty ladies.

Elgar

Qn: Elda, Helga. Elger. Elgar. Is your name Elgar?
Elgar: Yes.

Qn: Are you a musician? (No). A composer? (Maybe). You are going to have to be a bit more specific please.
Elgar: Not musician as such. But I did compose for a bit.

Qn: Can you tell us about your nationality for confirmation.

---

107 He married twice. Not sure who the third is that he referred to and possibly dodged?

Elgar: I am a well-travelled individual.

Qn: Are you Elgar, the famous composer? (No response). Are you being modest, did you write any well-known pieces? (Yes). And were these pieces played in Europe? (Yes).

Qn: Are you a 19th century composer? (Yes). Did you compose some thumping overtures?
Elgar: No, my music does not thump. It rouses.

Qn: Are you here for a reason? (Yes). What reason and what is your favourite composition?
Elgar: To see you. My favourite was a small piece written for my goddaughter. It was entitled the life beyond the boundaries and included animals, birds, and rivers, these majestic flowers, not like you know here, but smaller and wild.

Qn: How do you listen to modern music in the physical world?
Elgar: With my soul.

Qn: Have you had other lives, Elgar? (Yes). Would you share one with us?
Elgar: I have walked on this plane before. Child and man. My behaviour was not always as I would have liked, but that's all part of learning, is it not.

Qn: Have you lived as other cultures?
Elgar: Three. A child, a boy, and a man. Three stages, but I think there is four stages, an older man.

Qn: Last question then. Are you a very old Spirit? (Yes). What Level are you at?
Elgar: I am a Level 7.

Finally, during the VE80 remembrance celebrations we were visited by Andrew the day before I planned to submit the final manuscript to the publisher. I felt compelled to include the transcript of this brief conversation.

Andrew

Visitor: Good day.

Qn: Can you introduce yourself to us?
Visitor: My name is Andrew.

Qn: Are you Australian? (Yes). How did I know that? Because you said good day.
Andrew: Oh shucks.

B: What brings you here?
Andrew: Just to say hello. Have you been having good weather and plenty of of milk?

Qn: I am intrigued why an Australian is here. Is there a reason?
Andrew: Yes. I wanted to come. I don't hold you being a pom against you.

Qn: LOL. Were you here for an event? (80 year). Are you here for the remembrance celebration?
Andrew: Victory In Europe.

Qn: Did you fight in Europe?
Andrew: We split and covered a lot like your comrades and all did.

Qn: Have you got any recollection that you wish to share?
Andrew: It is not a pleasant thing to remember war. But we fought valiantly with the English and the Americans in the Pacific.

Qn: Did you survive the war and go back to Australia? (Yes). You went home a hero.
Andrew: No, it was difficult to adjust back. People don't understand. When you are seeing your being exposed to the brutality of war it is hard to just return and carry on as if we had never been away. That believe it or not is what some people expected.

Thank you on behalf of all the people today for helping to keep the world free.

Karma

Karma is frequently characterised as the sum of an individual's actions throughout their current and previous lives. For proponents of reincarnation, karma may also be regarded as a determining factor for an individual's future existence. Consequently, one may inquire how karma is perceived within the spirit realm.

Qn: For individuals with a physical disability, it has been suggested that this is a payback for problems in past lives. Is this true?
Chief: No. It may be their path, their lesson. Not payback, but sometimes karma dictates.

Qn: Do we carry karma?
Chief: The sins of our fathers for small babies, are not their sins but the previous karma of the newborn's life from before. You can see that it would affect their next existence, not the sin as such, that is white, but the karma they carry is not. Sometimes it can take many visits to improve the state of latent karma.

Qn: Why should a spirit wish to return to another physical life to remove the karma?
Conglomerate: Some come down as they have made a bit of a hash of their previous existence. They came down to follow a path, but something happened. They took a sideways path. They didn't get to the important parts. They had left undone what they wished to achieve. So, they come down for a second chance to complete it

and once it is completed, they are at peace. I understand from your Guide, you carried with you some karma and if it was not for you coming down this time, you would still have that guilt and karma with you.

Qn: But how does the karma weigh down a spirit in the Light?
Conglomerate: Because it is there as a burden. When you go back into spirit, you become acutely aware, more aware than you are here. If you are sad about something or that something didn't happen, guilt is the usual karma. Guilt about something you had or had not done in your physical life, and it weighs on you. Even in the spirit world, where most burdens are lifted, it weighs still upon your conscience. So, sometimes you need to return to the physical world and work through that karma and learn to understand why or what happened, or to make up for what happened. It is often difficult for one to know exactly what one needs to do. But when you talk with the planners, when you discuss the scenarios that would help to relieve you, what you need to come down and work through, they can arrange for you to be in a situation where you can work through or understand what you are worried about or feeling the burden of.

It is difficult for you to understand, but when you live in an area where there is perfection, if you do not feel perfect yourself, it can weigh upon you. You wish to feel perfect, you wish to feel good. If you have in your heart a weight of remorse because you are aware of your life and you know what you have done and lived in your life, and you know what guilt you take because you have not been able to rectify it in your life, you cannot take guilt into the world of spirit. In the physical world there is no need to worry. Physically rectified automatically.

But because you are human, and even when you go into spirit you are still human, you carry your feelings with you. They do not leave you; they will go with you. You do not lose your identity, whichever one it is you choose to pick. You do not lose your identity; you remain yourself and carry with you the burdens. Those unfinished businesses, some are so petty that you can see from above that they have rectified themselves. I am talking about the major things, the more major incidents that can affect people, that guilt does not go away. If you have done something as a child or a teenager, that guilt does not go away. It's still there and every now and again, well imagine if you have the memories of accessing lifetimes of information. Those karma can build up and need to be removed. You need to work through them, either repent them or come to terms with them.

A *Physical* Life Path

It is intriguing to learn that many spirits choosing to come back down to the physical world do so with a pre-determined life path plan. Initially, I found this concept challenging to comprehend, especially considering that an individual's memories are erased prior to reincarnating into the new physical body. Furthermore, if the life path is pre-determined, it raises the question of how the individual knows what they must accomplish when they are unable to access their higher consciousness where these memories are stored.

On certain occasions, members of the Circle would request the Chief to select a topic for discussion. On this particular occasion, the Chief elected to address the Circle regarding the convergence of life paths and their potential interconnections between individuals.

"Chief: I am sure that all I have shown you is relevant to your lives and after lives. You will be surprised that all the things you have learnt are relevant to the life you lead, also to the lives you have led in the past, and the lives to come. How, you may ask yourself and me. Well, if you pay attention I will explain.

You see, all your lives interweave, and this is pre-destined; through the course of time and effort you will see that what I say is truth. You can lead the life you think is best for you, but life changes; and your past returns to you with those you may only have fleeted grasp of,[108] redirecting your life plan back on course so that you will once again be back on your desired course of direction. You may only see this person for a short time span in your existence, but they have disturbed your headed trajectory, and it changes the course and outcome. That lucky chance destined meeting, it turns you onto the course or path you should be on. There are these planned pre-destined meeting points throughout your existence, they are like signposts and help to keep you on track. You also will have pre-programme meeting points in your planned existence; most times all works well. We have back-up points should one point fail to materialise; and you should have seen that before your existence begins in the physical. Thus, your route."

Qn: Is that for everyone or only for those who may have special tasks?
Chief: All have basic plans. Some more complex, obviously. Yours is...

Qn: Is that a pre-programmed activity?
Chief: You had two objectives hastily added, because you fell down[109] so to speak. Your objectives have been less planned and more freelanced ... but with your karma you have at last worked out some of ... from the past lives. You have also begun the messaging that was required by us all; an important job, for it will be read by those that need it, and you will find that people will express their thoughts, and their minds will begin to open. That crack will produce all that is required to open people's minds to their possible future when their path comes to the Veil between this life and your home.

---

108 'Fleeting grasp of' is the Chief referring to those people whom we may think we are meeting for the first time in a current physical existence but who we may find we share affinities or objectives with that could also be due to associations from past lives or in spirit.

109 This was explained and the confidential information relating to the individual has been excluded.

Qn: Does this mean you were predestined to cross our path, to nudge us a bit further along our way.
Chief: Yes. I am always looking after this Circle, and I am here as one of those points to further illustrate what I mean about what has been said previously. I am trying to help broaden your knowledge and help with the writing.

ॐ

Visitors to the Circle often wanted to know more about why they might have returned to the physical world and their chosen life path. However, it was often the case that spirits typically hesitated to provide such information to avoid influencing or making decisions on behalf of individuals regarding their life choices. However, an individual's spirit Guides may provide subtle guidance at various points during their lifetime, which could be interpreted as the signposts mentioned by the Chief in his address. An individual's life path is a personal matter, and understanding this concept may help others comprehend their own choices.

Qn: How can you tap into your soul's purpose?
Conglomerate: This being the purpose that one has come down to the physical for.

The whole point of your purpose is a journey through this life which will lead you to something that you wish to learn. You see, you have free choice all the way along when you come into the physical world and in the spirit world. So, if we sent you down here and said, this is your map, look at it, study it, take it with you, every time you come to a question you would not be free to make that choice because you would unroll your map. So, if you were constricted in what you could do where would the learning be in that. You would just be following a map and would be walking to wherever the map said. You would never learn that if you went the other way it was a bit rough and steep, and it may have been better to walk another way. You would never learn these things.

A roadmap is with you, but you cannot use it. Your Guides can use it, they can guide you gently and give you instincts to follow this path, and this is a lot better for you but of course you have free choice so you may choose not to listen to that instinct. It is down to you to work out that path with the help of your Guides because then you would have obtained the full learning and experience here. Otherwise, you would be forever looking at life through the lens of a camera and not experiencing life. Your life would become limiting because you are only looking and following this map. There are good reasons why we don't allow you access to those maps so easily.

Qn: Do we choose our intent and are we guided to areas that suit our skills, or can we choose our intent.
Conglomerate: You can choose your intent[110], but your Guides will help to guide you. Should you have a desire before you come down to obtain something, they will help to guide you to it. If on the other hand, you decide that you did not wish that path, you have the absolute decision. You can decide your path and they will do their best to bring you back to the right path. So, you may find that you go around in circles quite often if you are not on the right path. So, it is up to them to help you to get to the path that you have set for yourself. But yours is the decision.

After committing to writing this book, I had a meeting with a spiritual Medium not associated with the Library Circle. She disclosed that I had something important to complete and was

---

110   Your life path.

surrounded by energy. At the next Circle sitting, I asked for clarification from my spirit Guides...

Qn: What was this thing about being surrounded?
John: All of us, we bring energy to you. Life is important and we like to help wherever possible so that you all experience the best that you can and also that you follow your paths as best we can make it for you. You all find that there are times when you feel a little pushed on and give you space and inclination to follow a way that will coincide with your paths. How many times have you felt a little lost and you feel bereft of direction, you will need to sit and ask – "Please give me a little guidance, perhaps a little shove in the right direction." We all find that things in this world cause us disquiet, for example pain. But it does not take long, and the rewards are worth the effort, so to speak.

When you work with and for spirit, and we work with and for you, then all the time there is the possibility that unforeseen things will come along where extra help may be required. You have dedicated some of your existence to certain work with the word and love and light in this world, I can categorically tell you now that you all are signed up to this work before you left your home to venture down here.[111]

---

111   This message was addressed to all in attendance.

Energy and Bumps and Bangs

A lot has already been said about how spirits can utilise energy for various purposes within their dimension, however one can only speculate whether spirits can also manipulate energy to affect physical activities on the Earth plane. Communication and spiritual healing are two areas where there is evidence of such impact. Furthermore. maybe some readers have heard unexplained knocks from within a house or room that is distinct from sounds produced by central heating systems. I am referring to knocks that appear to originate from solid wooden objects or furniture rather than that which can be associated with temperature changes.

In a previous residence, we would hear occasional bumps and bangs, which I often attributed to the expansion and contraction of metal pipes serving the central heating system that occurred even during the summer months when the system was not in use. Several years ago, we moved to a newly constructed house equipped entirely with PVC piping, however the bumps and bangs persisted, so I eventually got around to asking whether these sounds could be manifestations of spirits indicating their presence.

Qn: Can you tell us more about how spirit uses energy?
Chief: I will do my best to give some guidance on the matter of energy, and it's uses. I am not talking about the energy contained within your personal bases or that within most living objects in your

physical understanding, but that which is accessible for us to use in our working environment and space. Some objects store energy that can be used by the person or their Guides e.g. crystals. You see that we use the surplus energy brought by numbers of people to support certain items and demonstrations in the more advanced environment. If you find that energy is all around you, then it becomes easier to do bigger demonstrations. I think that some also can call on and sit in the Creators light whereby you have access to the Universe's energy source, which can fill any void and is more plentiful than anyone realises. The space around every area is filled with energy but the Creator's light is stronger and can be safely meditated within; the healing can come from that place.

Qn: Is it true that some objects store energy whilst other objects don't?
Chief: Yes. They were designed that way in the creation of them.

Qn: Are you talking about the storage of physical energy?
Chief: The type we can use in our spiritual being.

Qn: Can you tell us where the energy of the Light comes from?
Chief: The Light's energy comes from the Creator's Universe.

Qn: Do Spirits bring the energy of the Light with them to speak with us?
Chief: We ask. And it is funnelled towards us.

Qn: Is it better to use the Creator's energy or the energy drawn from us to work?
Chief: A mixture of both.

Qn: How do you bring the Creator's energy to this room?
Chief: We build it through our connection to the Light. Remember energy is all around us in every place. Some of it comes from the

Spirit Realm, and this connection and protection we call Creator's light and Creator's energy.

Qn: Is there just one Creator energy?
Chief: No. Other Creators have their own type of energy with a vibration suited to their needs. It all comes from the same Source.

Qn: Focussing on our Individual Source area, is there only one type of energy? (Yes). Can you use that energy for different things. (Yes). Do you adjust the energy to use it for different things?
Chief: Always. It will depend on what it is to be or be used for.

Qn: What is the difference between physical energy and healing energy?
Chief: Healing is on a different wavelength of vibration. For example, to grasp it easier, if you think of a rainbow made up of colours each made up of individual wavelengths, these could be split down into different uses. For example, red for physical, yellow for spiritual, blue for communication, green for the planet and all on and around etc. Does this help to picture it.

Qn: A little, still struggling. Any way you can simplify?
Chief: You still feel that it is difficult to understand how energy can change, when you have the simplest description available in the physical in your everyday lives; water. Where does the wet in your washing go? Where does the ice on the ground go? Let me explain, they are all to do with energy. The ice, as you know, is water, but it is solid. Give it heat and it excites the molecules breaking the solid bonds and turning it into a free moving liquid that you can still see, speed up the vibration by applying a little more heat and it gets more excited breaking away the liquid bonds that hold the water and turning it into gas that cannot be seen.

Qn: So, what you're describing is how energy can transpose itself from one state to another, and that we shouldn't be surprised. (Yes). It's the same energy, but with each change of vibration it becomes something else. (Yes). And your example also applies to us transitioning from physical back to spirit, whilst we remain the same?
Chief: Yes, can you understand my example.

Qn: How do you manifest bumps and bangs?
Chief: Easy. A build-up of energy within the fabric of the object.

Qn: What happens?
Chief: It is a bit like when you crack or click your joints. We crack the fibres of the object; they then return to normal minus the build-up of energy.

Qn: So, you must use an object.
Chief: Even if it's a gas.

Qn: Must these be objects that can hold energy?
Chief: Yes. We build up the energy within the fibres.

Qn: Is there any danger of breakage to the object when you do this?
Chief: No. Although saying that, we pose no danger to the object, but that does not mean those less practised than us could not destroy or break an object.

Qn: If you are the spirit doing this, are they exterior to the object? (Yes). Are they somehow manipulating the energy in the object.
Chief: You are thinking of us as a solid. Please remember, as we passed out of our bodies, we can pass through objects in our energy state.

Qn: So, do you work from within the object, when you do that? (Yes). Does that mean the whole of you has to be within the object? (No). Just part of you. (Yes). Is this because you can blend with all energy? (No). Can you explain how you do this using the drum as an example?
Chief: Yes. We move the drum by creating an energy cushion that enables us to manipulate the drum with very little resistance.

Qn: Are you exterior to that drum.
Chief: Part in the drum.

Qn: So, you might place your hand in the drum to move it. (Yes). And there is a current of energy around the drum for the drum to float on. (Cushion). And then you place a hand in the drum to move it as if you are writing. (Yes). How do you blend the hand into the drum.
Chief: Into its energy.

Qn: How do you do that if the energies are different?
Chief: We can adjust our vibration.

Qn: Do you use our energy to help you?
Chief: We could use your excess energy, but we prefer the energy from the Light that is also transmitted through yourselves.

Qn: Can you create a bump or a bang in thin air? (Yes). Without an object.
Chief: The air is an object, but not as effective.

Qn: Is air energy as well?
Chief: Everything is energy.

Qn: In theory you can do this with anything you want if it's energy.
Chief: No, not living things, because it would damage living things.

Qn: Can you create a puff of wind in the air? (Yes). To create a force out of nothing?

Chief: Yes. The energy can build up behind a molecule to create unequal pressure on one side causing the natural order of seeking the equilibrium to occur and that molecule will move, this in turn will create the next molecule to move and so on building if you apply enough energy.

General Questions

Below are answers to some general questions that just did not seem to fit in with the other Sections but may still be of interest to a reader.

Energy

Qn: How does an individual's energy change if they change Level?
Conglomerate: Your energy, as it develops, will become stronger, this is how it works. But I must say, not everybody progresses past the Level that they are in but may still become stronger within that Level. For they will have gained more experience but are not ready to progress beyond their Level, so they just develop stronger energy.

Qn: Do I control my spiritual energy, vibration, and colours?
Conglomerate: By choosing your path and by having achieved it in the past, that is how you develop. You do not get to say, I would like to be blue today, I would like to be red tomorrow, or I would like to be gold the next day. You have the colours that are you, these show what you have done with your life and your spirit. It is your record, your development and who you are.

Qn: 1 of 3 After physical death is the residue energy always kept as one, or can it be split up and distributed.
Conglomerate: By residue energy, I do not understand.

Qn: 2 of 3 The energy of the spirit. rather than residue energy when we die on this plane.
Conglomerate: We are the whole Spirit.

Qn: 3 of 3 Is it kept as one or can it be distributed?
Conglomerate: It is kept as one for that is your identity, your personality. It is your physical body that will disintegrate and return to natural energy to the ground, but your spirit energy will stay as one for it will be you, and you will be welcomed back into the spirit world as you are. For natural energy, expect to know that the physical body will feed others.

Qn: 1 of 3 How do you survive as energy if spirit does not eat?
Conglomerate: Because energy is never created nor destroyed, it is just redeployed.

Qn: 2 of 3 How do you continue to exist in spirit?
Conglomerate: In the Creators energy. We live in energy, we are energy. We draw our strengths from energy. Do not think that someone who loves a good meal is happy to give it up, we understand this. So, you create your own banquets, of course they will not taste the same, but you can remember what it tastes like, so you put the taste onto them. You can still enjoy a pint, you will not get the alcoholic kick, but you will still enjoy the flavour.

Qn: 3 of 3 Is the energy limitless?
Conglomerate: It never dies. There is a fundamental principle about energy that goes through the Universe. It is not created; it is not destroyed. It is redeployed.

Qn: What should we see when an energy form passes?
Conglomerate: I see the form that it is. For I can react faster than you. The human eye, while being a miracle of development, cannot

react fast enough to see our vibrations. The human eye does not react fast as it is always changing focus, it is how it is designed, whereas the camera will focus in one area and is stable, the human eye cannot maintain its stability as it is forever changing focus.

Soulmates

Qn: What are Soulmates?
Conglomerate: Soulmates are two spirits whose lights blend for eternity and are part of the one. One life lived with each other throughout time, not necessarily in the physical. Their spirits are bonded at the base level of spirituality, and this forms a bond that is felt deeper than friendship, that is beyond the realms of understanding by most. They do not spend all the time together, but when they come together it is known also that their parting will be keenly felt.

Spirit Activity

Qn: Why is it that spirit tends to be active more when it is dark?
Chief: We can be active in the daylight. But as you see with the transfigurations, they are harder to see as the daylight tends to dissipate[112] the Energy a bit, so for action in the daylight you need to have more participants or need to have a natural build-up energy in a larger quantity.

Qn: What colour is your energy? (Light). *Where do you gain your light from?*
CP: The Veils. When you go through the Veils you gain energy, you

---

[112] The energy used for transfiguration is grey and clear that can usually be seen in red light within a dimly lit room. It is unlikely that a transfiguration will be seen in natural daylight.

boost your available abilities. For example, here you can come from any Level due to your specialism, and you can progress your skills and advance through the Levels obtaining more ways to help. It is learning, and you benefit from this learning. Also, by coming down to the physical you learn to relate to others when they suffer. This does not occur in spirit much, so you need to come down to further understand the suffering of your fellow man to progress your healing Guide existence and become better at what you take with you into your next life.[113]

Time

Qn: Can you explain the infinity symbol and how time differs between the two worlds?
Chief: I will. There is a symbol that means all of time and distance. You may think that analogy is quite strange, but you see, time is infinite so the measure of it is not really possible. On Earth, you only measure the passing of the sun and moon, and this also applies to your seasons that you measure by the nature world around you. You must understand these are not fixed times in the Universe only on this speck of a planet. You create your own treadmill, and you create your own timescale which helps your existence but only applies to this speck of dust in the Universe. If you disregard this time constraint you will get more of an understanding of what your home life is like when you return to spirit.

Animals and Plants

Qn: Can spirit people come back to the physical as animals?
Conglomerate: It is unusual for this to happen because although you

---

[113] The member asking this question is a retired Nurse who is specialising and developing her healing skills.

are all spiritual energy, you are all different types of spirits. You are, so to speak, the top of the food chain and this is quite difficult to go and change completely. You understand that the spirit as an animal is completely different, it is a different vibration to human.

Qn: Are plant life and human life different?
Conglomerate: Yes. They are different energies.

Language

Qn: Is there a spoken language in the spirit world?
CP: Yes, it is universal, no matter what language is spoken.

Qn: Does that mean that you have like a unique translation?
CP: Yes, we hear in our understanding.

Qn: Could we understand this language if spoken now.
CP: You will when you return home.

Qn: Is this a kind of Light language?
CP: Yes, it is a spirit language from the start of the Creation.

Council

Qn: Is your Conglomerate part of a Council that may make decisions about the Earth plane?
Conglomerate: Let us put it this way. We are not one of the Prophets. But we do our best to supply knowledge and we may be called upon very, very occasionally. When we have been called, how wonderful, and it is just for a little bit of information that we can supply. But we do not make the decisions, it is not our position. It is for those on the highest Levels to make the decision about the Earth. There are those nearer to the Earth that make decisions about various

mundane things, like who the Guides are going to be, which life are you going to go into, what is it that you wish to attain, what is it you wish to experience, are you happy going there, do you think you can cope with that life, could it bring you what you want to know, could it bring you what you want to learn. These are more everyday mundane, but the higher decisions are made a lot higher, you would expect that.

It is a great privilege to be called before the Council to be involved, even in just a smidgen of a way is a great privilege. Of course, the main Teacher does the talking then, it is his rank, and he has seniority. But we all attend together as one group, and if he does not know, he is not so proud that he does not turn to one of us and says this is your field can you lend assistance. Of course, we step up to say I can help, I can offer this advice; I can offer this information.

Conundrum

Although I am confident that our conversations with spirits will continue in the foreseeable future, I admit to being unsure of the form they will take, what will be said, or who we may be visited by, apart from our regular spirit visitors. Engaging with spirits can be full of surprises, which I hope remains the case as it is a wonderful experience. When I commenced writing this book, I had little idea of the information that would emerge from the spirit world, and I do not foresee any change in this dynamic, nor would I desire it to change. Through these communications, I have come to appreciate the profound wisdom and insights shared by our spirit visitors. Each encounter has deepened my understanding of the afterlife and the intricate connections between our physical existence and the spiritual realm. The knowledge imparted by these spirit visitors has been both illuminating and comforting, offering glimpses into the mysteries and curiosities of the spirit world as it really is and without influence of any type.

Over the years, I have found myself in awe at the intricate balance that exists between the physical and spiritual worlds. This delicate balance is rooted in the essence of our existence and shapes our understanding of our place in the Universe, regardless of individual faith or belief. As one delves deeper into these spiritual communications, it becomes apparent that the information provided by our spirit visitors transcends all cultural and religious boundaries. It offers a universal truth that speaks to the core of our being, highlighting the interconnectedness and shared energy that flows through all living things. This energy unites us and provides continuity and purpose as we navigate the complexities of physical existence.

Some readers may come to realise that the knowledge that has been shared with us is not only enlightening but also deeply reassuring. It provides comfort and hope as we continue our journey through an ever-changing physical world, sometimes for better, sometimes for worse. The insights gained from these interactions have enriched my understanding of the afterlife and enhanced my appreciation of the delicate interplay between our physical and spiritual selves.

I had hoped to convey information that might offer greater understanding and awareness of the intrinsic links between the spirit and physical worlds, and how we might perceive spirits given the ever-growing scientific knowledge of the Universe in the 21st century. It has taken me many years and much patience to gather the information that has been presented in the preceding Sections, but I trust the words of the spirits who worked closely with me to answer the many questions posed by the Circle about the afterlife that we will all eventually return to. I think that I have succeeded.

As I approached the final section of this book, I pondered how best to conclude it. This is not a story with a happy ending or a twist. There was no need for concern, as the Chief conveyed an unusual message and posed a conundrum, requesting that it be communicated to the readers in the final section.

Chief: Where, if you could go anywhere, would you go?
It is interesting the way that the physical works. It dreams outside itself, but this is not always possible, but nevertheless, our spirit yearns for more satisfaction, and this is normal because you are not used to being tied to your physical body when you descend to Earth. This physical life is not your reality and, somewhere inside your spirit you

remember that this is so, and you dream of more than you can have in the physical world. I do not mean ambition; I mean a deep feeling or longing for certain things attached to memories of old. This world is built on memories and understanding of the spirit. You are not sent totally blind to this Earth; you still carry the innovation of the many times you have been before. Note I do not say knowledge, only you know innovation. You, all through your allotted lives here, are given self-chosen goals to fulfil, but as you have free choice you also add to the programme as you progress through this life. So, you have a path, but that path can be as wide in places or as narrow allowing for choice to be made. You can choose your side activities, but who is to say these are also on your path due to your inner backward fixtures lodged within your body's spirit memories.

There is a conundrum for you to ponder on, what came first?

Some of us will shape our lives and world around whether they are in the physical world or in the spirit world. So, do you bring from the spirit world the ideas to adjust and transform this physical world or do you take back from this physical world to adjust where you are living[114] in the spirit world. What do you think?

While I do not have the definitive answer to this question, I have formed my own views of what came first. That said, I very much prefer to leave for the reader to reflect and decide what you think. Regardless of your view, it is important to go about your life with care in this physical world and strive to be kind, considerate, and compassionate during your time here, and to avoid Karma.

---

114   The Chief is referring to when you eventually return home to the infinite existence that awaits in the spirit world, and where you will have lived for the most part of your existence.

In concluding this book, it is my sincere hope that you have found some value in the conversations presented in this book, and the insights from the contributions of various spirits. If they have succeeded in opening minds to the possibilities of the afterlife, then the effort has been worthwhile.

Other Life in the Universe

The answers provided by spirits to questions about the physical Earth, the spirit world, and their sustenance by the energy of the Universe have, I hope, enhanced the readers' understanding of some of the interconnections between the physical and spiritual realms. Both can be acknowledged as integral and essential parts of a much broader Universe that has developed over billions of years. We have been told that the Universe, is composed of different forms of energy and holds limitless potential for the emergence or creation of other life forms from those energies. Consequently, most people should be able to acknowledge that there are many possibilities for other physical and/or spiritual life structures to evolve somewhere else in the Universe.

We live in an era that is characterised by significant advances in scientific knowledge and technology. Therefore, it should not come as a surprise when scientists and astronomers assert that there could be over 100 billion stars and 200 billion planets in our galaxy alone; this is considered to be a conservative assessment of the Milky Way galaxy, where our Solar System is located. Astronomers also estimate that the observable Universe, the part visible through the most powerful telescopes, contains approximately two hundred sextillion (200,000,000,000,000,000,000,000) stars[115]. Given these

---

115 This number is not fixed and seems to be subject to change as astronomers look further into the Universe, which is expanding all the time.

astronomical numbers, there must be a high likelihood that Earth is not the only planet in this galaxy or the Universe capable of sustaining physical and spiritual life forms. Additionally, some scientists and astronomers claim that the Universe may comprise upwards of 200 billion[116] galaxies. Given these factors, the creation of life in the Universe is unlikely to have occurred solely on Earth. Furthermore, the images published from the James Webb telescope provide visual evidence of the vastness and diversity of celestial bodies in the Universe all created from energy.

If there are other life forms that exist in other galaxies. or within our own galaxy, they are likely to be so far away from Earth that travel between the two inhabited worlds is most likely beyond the physical capabilities of humans or any technologically advanced 'Star People' life forms that may exist elsewhere in the Universe. Within the Milky Way the brightest and closest star to Earth is Sirius, which is assessed to be 8 light years away from Earth. If scientists currently working on new innovative ways to use light to travel to other planets succeed, it is estimated that it might still take 69 years to reach Sirius. Alpha Centauri, half the distance at 4 light years away, is not as bright, and it could take 140 years to travel there using similar technology. When Voyager 1 was launched in 1977 scientists estimated that it would take 40,000 years for Voyager 1 to reach Alpha Centauri using the technology of the 1970s. Given that reaching those two closest stars will take beyond human lifetimes travelling at the speed of light, contact with other life forms in the Universe remains a very unlikely scenario for now. Or is it?

---

116 This is a minimum estimate given by astronomers. The upper estimate is higher and continues to be updated the further they can see into the Universe.

You may recall the conversation with the Conglomerate relating to the Source where it was mentioned that other distinct sources of creation exist, which can sustain planetary life forms within their respective domains. If the Universe is comprised of energy and all life existing within it consists of various degrees or bandwidths of this vibrating energy, it is reasonable to hypothesise that there is life elsewhere in the Universe beyond Earth. If these areas or galaxies contain planets capable of sustaining life at different stages of development, it is also likely that another galaxy older than the Milky Way could have physical or spiritual life forms on one of its planets, perhaps with physical life or technological development that is beyond human understanding. However, if they are made up of similar structures of energy, is it theoretically possible for these Star People, or their energy, to communicate with the spiritual energy in our spirit realm by using these so-called energy lines to communicate and travel...

www.ingramcontent.com/pod-product-compliance
Lightning Source LLC
Chambersburg PA
CBHW020758160426
43192CB00006B/368